I0824172

PRAISE FOR A SPOONFUL OF EVERYWHERE

"*A Spoonful of Everywhere* is your passport to global flavor, brought to life with warmth, authenticity, and culinary mastery. A must-have for anyone who believes the kitchen is where the world comes together."

—Chef Dean Fearing, The Ritz-Carlton Dallas

"Whether you know Abraham from his glorious restaurant, Salum, or meet him here for the first time, this book will leave you enchanted and craving more."

—Lee Cullum, columnist, *The Dallas Morning News*

"This gorgeous book captures what makes Abraham and Salum so special: soulful flavors, generous hospitality, and dishes you'll want to make again and again."

—D'Andra Simmons, entrepreneur, television personality, and culinary judge

A SPOONFUL OF EVERYWHERE

SALUM
RESTAURANT
Open
103

A SPOONFUL OF EVERYWHERE

An Immigrant Chef's Journey Through Global Cuisine

Abraham Salum
Chef/Owner of Salum

with James O. Fraioli

Photography by Alejandra Urquiza

Skyhorse Publishing

Culinary Book Creations

Skyhorse Publishing books may be purchased in bulk at special discounts for sales promotion, corporate gifts, fund-raising, or educational purposes. Special editions can also be created to specifications. For details, contact the Special Sales Department, Skyhorse Publishing, 307 Fifth Avenue, 4th Floor, New York, NY 10016 or info@skyhorsepublishing.com.

Visit our website at www.skyhorsepublishing.com.

Culinary Book Creations LLC
www.culinarybookcreations.com

10 9 8 7 6 5 4 3 2 1

Library of Congress Cataloging-in-Publication Data available on file.

Production: James O. Fraioli, Culinary Book Creations LLC
Cover photograph by Alejandra Urquiza Photography
Designers: theBookDesigners

Print ISBN: 978-1-5107-8603-5
Ebook ISBN: 978-1-5107-8728-5

Printed in China

To My Father,
You taught me to treat everyone with respect,
to love without conditions,
and to see the world without judgment.
Those lessons became the recipe
for how I live, cook, and love.
I carry you in me forever.

CONTENTS

Soup of the Day
Cup 5.50 Bowl 7.00
Salum House Salad
Field Greens, Balsamic Dijon
Vinaigrette, Red Onions and
Spiced Pecans
Cobb Salad
Shrimp 20

LUNCH MENU
JUNE 2025
SMALL PLATES
Texas Goat Cheese
Roasted Elephant Garlic and
Virgin Olive Oil
Mussels, App 18
Belgian Style Beer,
and Garlic Aioli
Made Country Pâté
Mustard, Cornichons and
— 18
Roasted Red
Candied
— 18

FOREWORD

by JENNIFER FRANKLIN
Atlanta-based author

I remember the first time I met Abraham. He was a guest chef at a food festival in Mexico's Mayan Riviera, which I was covering as a journalist. Our husbands quickly bonded over being in paradise while we worked, and they encouraged us to meet. That night, amid the chaos of hungry festivalgoers searching for their next bite, Abraham stood out—joyful, focused, and calm. It's rare to feel such an instant soul connection, but with Abraham, I did. We became kindred spirits almost immediately.

Since then, I've treasured our time together—wandering markets in Mexico, sharing fine dining in his hometown of Dallas, sitting at a chef's table in Atlanta, and walking through the Peruvian Andes. But one experience in Aguas Calientes, the town at the base of Machu Picchu, revealed his true approach to food. After climbing to the Sun Gate before dawn, we returned to town exhausted and hungry. Instead of settling for the first restaurant we found, Abraham insisted we search for something remarkable—the right meal to match the wonder of the day. I don't remember the name of the restaurant, but I'll never forget the joy of bright ceviche and Lomo Saltado with perfectly seared beef and crisp potatoes. It wasn't just a meal; it was discovery.

That day showed me Abraham's philosophy. For him, food is never about showing off or being overly complicated. It's about creating moments of genuine excellence. Whether savoring a traditional dish in a remote village or sharing a recipe he's crafted for home cooks, his joy for cooking is always present—and contagious.

That same spirit infuses every page of *A Spoonful of Everywhere*. His multicultural upbringing, passion for authentic flavors, and thoughtful storytelling shine through, making his recipes both approachable and inspiring. I know you'll enjoy cooking from this book—and you may find, as I did, that this dynamic, big-hearted chef becomes your kindred spirit too.

INTRODUCTION

Roots in Mexico City

I was born and raised on Calle Providencia in Colonia del Valle, Mexico City, an old neighborhood built in the 1920s. It surrounded me with rich cultural influences where my world revolved around family, friends, and food. My Mexican, Italian, Spanish, and Lebanese heritage further shaped my upbringing.

When I think of food, I believe my palate for the finer things began almost as soon as I entered the world. My mother, Leticia Elia Eleonora Cerdeño Mateos—known to everyone simply as "Hompy"—loved to share a particular story. When I was eight months old, I held a cracker topped with Roquefort cheese. Apparently, I would lick off the cheese and toss the cracker aside. Mom was amazed that such a young child had a taste for bold flavors. Since then, I've never been a picky eater. I'll try anything at least once—snake wine in Vietnam, fish scales in Japan, or insects in Mexico. Keeping my mind (and palate) open to new experiences has shaped me as a cook and continues to inspire me every day.

A House Always Full of Food

Our home in Mexico was always buzzing with life—family and friends dropping by unannounced, with everything centered around food. Celebrations were never small; uncles, cousins, neighbors, and friends of friends all gathered around the kitchen table.

New Year's Eve was especially legendary—sometimes themed, sometimes not—but always filled with laughter, music, and a "small" crowd of thirty or more who often stayed into the early hours. No one ever stepped into our home without being offered something to eat or drink.

Though my parents weren't big drinkers, they always kept a full bar, along with fresh fruit waters and delicious snacks for guests. One of the most beloved traditions was serving Lebanese coffee, followed by my father reading the coffee grounds to tell fortunes. To this day, friends still talk about how uncannily accurate he was—and how much we all miss his warmth, humor, and quiet magic.

Meals, Mothers, and Grandmothers

Daily meals growing up were simple: a bit of soup like fideo, spinach, or my favorite—squash blossom—some kind of protein, often fish, meat, or pork, and a crisp green salad. My mother adored salads, so they were always on the table. Our food wasn't heavily seasoned and, admittedly, often overcooked.

My mother didn't have much interest in cooking; her passions lay in painting, poetry, and golf. For her, the kitchen was more of a duty than a creative outlet. But while her meals were never elaborate, they were made with love. Luckily, I had two grandmothers whose cooking more than made up for what was missing at home.

Lilia: *Force of Nature*

My maternal grandmother, Lilia, stood under five feet tall and always told me, "Height is measured from your head to the heavens. So, I am taller than most people." Born in Tabasco in 1907, she lived through two world wars, revolutions, tragedies, and scandals. She left us at ninety-four, with no memory of any of it.

Her stories became family legend—like losing her mother at seven and taking over household duties, sewing clothes for her father and brother. Winning her favor was rare—and never permanent. There isn't a hurricane named after her that could match her force.

She lived with us, and I often peeked over her shoulder while she cooked, drawn to the aromas of garlic, onions, herbs, and spices. Her legendary dish was octopus stewed in its own ink. Those scents quietly shaped my soul.

Lilia also introduced me to opera. At seven years old, I sat through *Tristán e Isolda*—five hours in German—only to be rewarded with churros and hot chocolate at El Moro café afterwards. Soon, churros gave way to quail, foie gras, oysters, and suckling pig. She taught me how to strip a quail clean, why foie gras was such a delicacy, and how to taste the ocean in oysters. She showed me that food could transport us through time, memory, and place.

Amira: *The Pantry of Za'atar and Olives*

My paternal grandmother, Amira, the daughter of a Lebanese immigrant and an Indigenous Oaxacan woman, was equally remarkable. Born in Oaxaca in 1911, she mastered both Lebanese and Oaxacan cuisines.

As a college student, I visited her every Thursday for lunch. Even if I was her only guest, she prepared feasts: kibbeh nayyeh, tabbouleh, rice, stuffed grape leaves, labneh, and olives. She loved to cook for others, and I adored her. The scent of za'atar, olives, and fresh bread takes me back to her pantry instantly.

As a child, I would sneak in just to breathe in those aromas. She always cooked with ghee—her "special butter." Only years later did I learn the word "clarified butter" and understand its place in her cooking.

Becoming a Chef

In 1988, I realized I didn't want to study marketing—I wanted to be a chef. My father wasn't thrilled, but I secured an apprenticeship at the Camino Real Hotel in Mexico City, where I worked every station imaginable: dishwashing, polishing silver, garbage runs, room service.

I rotated through each kitchen—feeding three thousand at breakfast, learning strict French brigade structure at Fouquet's de Paris, navigating kosher rituals, and admiring the women who ran the cafeteria for two thousand employees with ease. Each station taught me discipline, teamwork, and respect for food's origins.

EXIT

That foundation carried me to the New England Culinary Institute in Vermont, where I survived endless snow, warmed myself (perhaps too faithfully) with Armagnac on my father's advice, and ultimately earned a place at L'Oustau de Baumanière in Provence. France changed me forever.

From there came Brussels, the Riviera Maya at Xcaret, San Antonio, Dallas, Parigi—and finally, opening Salum in 2005. Later, Komali became my tribute to authentic Mexican cuisine.

Travel has always been one of my greatest joys. Cooking in Argentina, Brazil, Spain, Oman, and Portugal . . . vacationing in Vietnam, Cambodia, India, and Nepal . . . each place shaped me as a person and as a chef.

Food memories are everywhere: tasting anchovies in Spain, cheese in France, parrilleros grilling over coals in Argentina, or monks offering blessings before a meal in Nepal. Whether a Michelin-starred tasting menu in Sydney or a squash blossom quesadilla in a Mexican market, every experience reminds me that food is connection.

Why This Book

One of my culinary instructors once told me: there are only two kinds of cuisine—good and bad. Start with the best ingredients, treat them with respect, and let love guide the process. That advice has never left me.

Writing this book has been one of the most personal journeys of my life. For years, I've shared food with guests at Salum, watching laughter and memories unfold. Now, through these pages, I get to share that same experience with you—right in your own home.

This book was born from countless conversations with guests, from family traditions, from my travels and mentors. More than a collection of recipes, it's an invitation: to cook with curiosity, to savor discovery, and to share food with those you love.

So, open these pages with excitement. Let's cook with heart, with soul, and with generosity. Let's bring people together around your table, creating moments that linger long after the last bite. Food tells our story—and it's always better when we share it.

CONTINENTAL INGREDIENTS & PANTRY

One of the things I love most about cooking with the seasons—and especially cooking here in Texas—is how much the ingredients can speak for themselves. We're lucky to have incredible local produce, proteins, and pantry staples right at our fingertips. My take on continental cuisine also draws from a wide range of global influences, from Mexican and Spanish to Lebanese and South Indian. Some of the ingredients I use are likely already in your kitchen, while others might be a little less familiar. Below is a primer on the more distinctive pantry staples featured throughout this book: what they are, how I like to use them, and where you might be able to find them. Use it as a guide—and a bit of inspiration—when building your own flavorful pantry.

Achiote (Annatto) Paste

Achiote paste is one of those powerhouse ingredients I always keep on hand. Made from annatto seeds, garlic, vinegar, and spices, it brings a bold, earthy depth and that unmistakable red-orange color I love—especially in dishes like the Slow-Roasted Yucatecan Pork with Sour Orange, Achiote & Red Onions (page 236) and the Redfish Wrapped in Banana Leaves with Citrusy Achiote Sauce (page 288). It's sold in dense little bricks (usually around 3.5 ounces), and for the recipes in this book, you can just break off what you need with a spoon. You'll usually find it in the Latin foods aisle at the grocery store, at Mexican markets, or online.

Agave Nectar

I reach for agave nectar when I want a touch of sweetness that's smooth, subtle, and a little more nuanced than sugar. A natural sweetener derived from the agave plant, it has a mild, floral sweetness and a smooth texture. It dissolves easily in both hot and cold liquids, making it a favorite in dressings, desserts, and of course, cocktails—you'll find its whisper of sweetness lends amazing flavor to the Crazy World Cantarito

Annatto Seeds

(page 30) and Desert Rose (page 33) sippers in my cocktail section. You can find it near the honey or natural sweeteners section in most grocery stores.

Banana Leaves

Banana leaves are one of my favorite ways to cook fish or meat—they gently steam whatever's inside while adding a subtle, grassy aroma you can't quite replicate any other way. I use them in my Yucatecan-Style Redfish recipe (page 288), where they help keep the fish tender and infused with flavor. You'll find banana leaves in the freezer section of most Latin or international grocery stores. Just thaw them before using, and if they feel stiff, a quick pass over an open flame or hot pan will make them more pliable for wrapping.

Cajeta (Dulce de Leche)

Cajeta is one of those ingredients I fell for the first time I tasted it—rich, velvety, and just tangy enough thanks to the goat's milk. It's like dulce de leche, but with a little more character. I use it to drizzle over fruit or even a scoop of vanilla ice cream. Look for it in Latin markets or online—it's usually sold in jars or squeeze bottles.

Chaat Masala

Chaat masala is one of those punchy spice blends that wakes up whatever you sprinkle it on. It's tangy, salty, a little funky—in the best way—and adds an unexpected pop to everything from fruit to fried snacks. I use it as part of the coating for the Crispy Spice-Coated Okra that accompanies the South Indian Lentil & Tomato Rasam on page 106, where it brings just the right hit of brightness and depth. You can find it at Indian grocery stores or online.

Chicharrónes

Chicharrónes are one of my favorite secret weapons for adding big flavor and serious crunch. These crispy pork rind cracklings aren't just for snacking—they make a killer topping, especially on dishes like the Smoky-Spicy Deviled Eggs with Crispy Cracklings and Red Chile Salsa (page 204). That salty, airy crunch brings the whole bite together. You'll find them in the snack aisle or sometimes near the butcher counter at Latin grocery stores. Grab a bag—you'll be surprised how often you reach for them.

Chili Peppers: *Fresh & Dried*

I'm obsessed with chiles. Fresh, dried, smoky, fruity, mild, or fiery—they're essential in Latin and Southwestern cooking, and they show up in just about every recipe in this book. (Quite literally: I counted over 75 references!) You'll usually find fresh chiles in the produce aisle, and a whole world of dried varieties like pasilla, guajillo, and árbol at Mexican markets or the spice section. These peppers are the backbone of so many sauces, soups, and stews here—building layers of flavor that keep things interesting.

Demi-Glace: *Beef, Lamb & Veal*

I rely on demi-glace constantly—it's a beautifully reduced stock, usually from beef, lamb, or veal bones, that adds serious umami punch to sauces and braises. You'll find it woven through the recipes, especially in dishes that balance savory and sweet, like the Rosemary-Thyme Wild Boar Chops with Blackberry Demi-Glace (page 272). While making it from scratch is rewarding, I often keep a high-quality pre-made version on hand—look for good brands in the freezer section or jarred near soup bases at specialty stores or online.

Epazote Leaves

Epazote is a bold, unmistakable herb I turn to when I'm slow-simmering beans or braises—it adds a unique, slightly pungent herbal flavor that you won't find anywhere else, plus it's traditionally known to help with digestion. You'll taste it in dishes like the Savory Pork Pozole Verde with Tomatillo, Jalapeño & Pepita Seeds (page 232). Fresh epazote is best found at Latin markets, but dried versions work well too for convenience. If you can't track it down, I usually substitute a mix of fresh Mexican oregano and cilantro in equal parts—it won't be quite the same, but it'll get you close.

Essential Oils: *Basil & Fennel*

I love working with culinary-grade essential oils like fennel and basil oil because just a drop or two can pack an incredible punch of concentrated flavor—perfect for lifting desserts, vinaigrettes, and syrups in unexpected ways. You'll find a few drops of basil oil bring a fresh, herbal lift to the honey drizzle on the Summer Berry, Mascarpone & Goat Cheese Tarts (page 54). Just make sure you're using food-safe oils—you can usually find them in the health or baking section of natural food stores, or easily online. Trust me, they're little flavor powerhouses worth having on hand.

Ground Chile Piquín Pepper

Ground chile piquín pepper brings instant fire and smoky heat to any dish. These tiny peppers pack a serious punch, and I love using the powder in rubs, spice blends, or to finish a dish with a bold kick. I especially love how it brightens up the Mayan Citrus Salad with Jicama, Grapefruit & Lime (page 71)—it's that perfect touch of heat that keeps the flavors dancing. You'll find it near the dried chiles at Mexican markets or spice aisles, but if you can't track it down, your favorite smoked chili powder makes a solid stand-in.

Hoja Santa

Hoja Santa adds complexity with its velvety texture and peppery, anise-like flavor. I love using fresh hoja santa leaves to wrap tamales or to infuse stews and soups with that unique twist. In this book, it plays a starring role in the filling for the Cremini Mushroom–Filled Chicken Roulades with Pine Nut Mole (page 196), where its subtle spice lifts the dish. You can find fresh hoja santa at Latin markets, but if you can't, dried versions work too—or try swapping in Mexican or French tarragon for a similar vibe.

Italian Cheeses: *Parmigiano-Reggiano & Pecorino Sardo*

I lean on Italian cheeses—particularly Parmigiano-Reggiano and Pecorino Sardo—whenever I want to add depth, salt, and that savory hit of umami to a dish. Parmigiano-Reggiano is nutty and complex, especially when aged, while Pecorino Sardo has a sharper, tangier edge that I love with vegetables or pasta. These cheeses show up all over this book—from Handmade Spinach-Potato Gnocchi (page 122) to Creamy Butternut Squash Bisque (page 118), plus in varying pesto sauces—because they're true foundational ingredients in my kitchen. When you're buying Parm, check for the stamped rind—that's how you know it's the real deal from Italy. And always, always buy it in a block and grate it fresh. The difference in flavor and texture is night and day.

Marcona Almonds

When it comes to nuts, Marcona almonds are one of my absolute favorites. Native to Spain, these little gems are rounder, softer, and naturally sweeter than regular almonds, with a buttery texture that adds a touch of luxury wherever they go. They always add flavor and crunch, especially in dishes like Fragrant Malbec-Poached Pears with Cabrales Cheese & Toasted Marcona Almond Purée (page 50) and Pan-Seared Scallops over Spinach Riso Pasta with Marcona Almond-Piquillo Butter Sauce (page 180). You can usually find them in the specialty nut aisle or imported foods section—grab a bag and keep them close.

Masa Harina

Masa harina is a cornerstone ingredient—it's a fine corn flour made from nixtamalized maize, which means the corn's been soaked in limewater to bring out its incredible flavor and texture. This is the magic behind soft, pliable dough for everything from tortillas to tamales and sopes. Here, masa harina even stars in the Sweet Chocolate-Date Tamales with Cinnamon (page 322), giving them that perfect tender bite. You'll find it in most grocery stores near the flour or Latin foods aisle—one pantry staple you'll want on hand.

Mexican Cheeses: *Manchego, Oaxaca, Asadero, Queso Fresco*

These Mexican cheeses are absolute workhorses in my kitchen. Each one brings something a little different to the table: Mexican-style Manchego is firm and nutty; Oaxaca is wonderfully stringy and melts like a dream; Asadero is creamy and mild, perfect for layering; and Queso Fresco is bright and crumbly—great for finishing a dish with a little contrast. You can usually find them in the cheese section of well-stocked grocery stores or at Latin markets.

Nopales

I love nopales for their bright, slightly tart flavor—kind of like green beans with a bit of snap. These prickly pear cactus paddles are super versatile, whether grilled, sautéed, or tossed fresh into salads. They really shine in the Lime-Kissed Nopales with Onions, Tomatoes, Cilantro & Chipotles (page 100), where their fresh, tangy bite takes center stage. You can find nopales fresh or jarred at Latin markets—both work great depending on what you're making.

Okra

I keep coming back to okra—not just for its mild, grassy flavor but also for the way its natural mucilage adds body and silkiness to stews and sauces. While it's a Southern staple, okra's versatility shines across global cuisines from Indian to West African. I love using it with the

Epazote Leaves

tangy punch of chaat masala as part of the crispy coating on fried okra (page 106)—a fun way to layer texture and spice. You'll find fresh or frozen okra in most produce sections, so it's easy to have on hand whenever inspiration strikes.

Piloncillo

I'll be honest, piloncillo might be one of my absolute favorite pantry staples. This unrefined cane sugar, usually sold in rustic little cones, brings deep molasses notes and earthy sweetness to everything it touches. Hence, it shows up all over the place, from savory standouts, especially desserts like the Mexican Chocolate Pecan Pie with Piloncillo Syrup (page 320), where it adds warmth and depth you just can't get from regular sugar. Also called papelón or panela, it's a cornerstone sweetener in Mexican cooking, with hints of vanilla, smoke, and spice. You'll find it at Latin grocers or online—usually in 1-ounce cones. Just grate it on a microplane or chop it finely.

Rasam Powder

This spice blend has serious soul. Rasam powder layers heat, depth, and tang with a mix of coriander, cumin, mustard seeds, black pepper, and sometimes a whisper of dried chile. It's what gives the South Indian Lentil & Tomato Rasam (page 106) its bold, unmistakable kick and aromatic complexity. I always keep some on hand—not just for rasam, but to punch up stews, roasted vegetables, even a quick tomato broth. Look for it at Indian grocery stores or online.

Saffron Threads

The delicate red stigmas of the crocus flower, saffron infuses dishes with a golden hue and floral aroma. It's floral, earthy, a little bitter, and it brings both elegance and intensity to anything it touches. It's the backbone of the Salum-Style Saffron Paella (page 151), a dish close to my heart, but you'll also find it turning up in some unexpected ways throughout these pages: like in the velvety saffron cream that cloaks seafood in the Squid Ink Pasta with White Wine–Kissed Seafood (page 172), or in the tomato-saffron sauce served beneath Za'atar-Crusted Halibut with Chickpea Croquettes (page 278). A little goes a long way—just a few threads bloomed in warm water or stock can change the entire direction of a dish. Look for high-quality saffron from Spain or Iran at spice shops or specialty grocers and treat it like gold—because it kind of is.

Tajin Seasoning

If you know, you know. This zesty chili-lime blend is a secret weapon in my pantry—and behind the bar. It brings a punch of brightness and just the right touch of heat, whether it's dusted over fruit slices or rimming a glass for one of the citrusy cocktails you'll find in this book. You'll spot it in the spice aisle or near the produce section in most grocery stores, and once you start using it, don't be surprised if it ends up on everything from roasted vegetables to grilled seafood.

Tamarind Pulp

Tamarind instantly wakes up a dish. It's sweet, sour, tangy, and deeply complex all at once. I use the pulp (either in paste or block form) to balance savory richness and add brightness to sauces, broths, and chutneys. You'll find it in the South Indian Lentil & Tomato Rasam, a dish that's practically a masterclass in layered flavor. Pick up tamarind pulp at most Latin or Asian grocers or online, and don't be afraid to experiment—it's far more versatile than you might think.

Truffle Peels

Truffle peels are one of my favorite secret weapons for layering in that unmistakable, earthy richness—without the cost (or pressure) of using fresh whole truffle. These paper-thin slices of black truffle, preserved in oil or brine, bring instant luxury to a dish. You'll taste them in the Panzanella Salad with Heirloom Tomato & Black Truffle Parmesan Crisps (page 148), where they add a savory depth to a summer classic, and again in the Dijon- and Truffle-Crusted Rack of Lamb (page 260), where they mingle with mustard and herbs to form a deeply aromatic crust. Look for them in jars or tins at gourmet shops or European markets.

Za'atar

This vibrant Middle Eastern blend—typically made with thyme, toasted sesame seeds, sumac, and salt—adds instant character and depth to meats, breads, and vegetables. Its herbal brightness and slight tang make it as versatile as it is craveable. In the Pan-Seared Halibut with Za'atar Crust on page 278, it forms a fragrant, textured layer that plays beautifully with the richness of the fish. Can't find it at your local grocer? That same recipe includes a quick DIY version so you can make your own from pantry staples.

KITCHEN TOOLS & EQUIPMENT

Here's a list of the essential tools I reach for repeatedly—trusty companions that help me bring the drinks and dishes in this book to life. Whether I'm crafting cocktails, frying fritters, or baking flan, having the right tool on hand makes the process smoother, more efficient, and—let's be honest—a lot more fun.

Basic Barware (Muddler, Shaker, Strainer)

This trio is the foundation of any good cocktail setup. I use a muddler to coax out the bright oils and juices from herbs and fruits, a shaker to bring everything together with the right chill and mix, and a strainer to keep things crisp and clean in the glass.

Cast Iron Skillets & Frying Pans

Cast iron is a staple in my kitchen. It holds heat beautifully and creates the kind of crust and sear that lighter pans just can't match. A large, heavy-bottomed skillet will become your go-to for everything from rustic cornbread to perfectly crisp empanadas.

Dutch Oven or Stockpot

This is one of my all-time favorite pieces of equipment. It's great for slow-simmered stews, deep-frying, braising—you name it. The even heat and tight-fitting lid help lock in flavor, and it transitions seamlessly from stovetop to oven.

Electric Mixer

Whether it's a stand mixer or a handheld one, this tool is a game changer for whipping cream, beating eggs, or kneading dough. I love the consistency it delivers—and it's a big help when your arm needs a break.

Fine Mesh Sieve

This humble tool pulls more weight than you'd think. I use it to strain sauces, sift flours, rinse grains—it's essential for achieving silky textures and clean finishes in both sweet and savory dishes.

Food Processor or High-Powered Blender

These are my workhorses. Whether I'm making mole, blitzing salsas, or emulsifying a sauce, one of these tools is almost always in play. If you're cooking your way through this book, you'll want at least one in your corner.

Ice Cream Scoop

Sure, it's great for dessert—but I also use it to portion out meatballs, fritters, and doughs. It keeps things even and tidy and helps things cook more uniformly. Once you try it, you'll never go back.

Immersion Blender

One of my favorite kitchen tools. It lets me blend soups and sauces right in the pot—no splatter, no extra cleanup. It's also perfect for aiolis, dressings, and anything small-batch that needs smoothness and speed.

Pasta Machine

If you're diving into the Mascarpone & Spring Pea Ravioli with Asparagus Pesto (page 162), a pasta machine will save your life—and your biceps. It rolls dough to a consistent thickness and helps you get that restaurant-quality finish at home.

Potato Ricer

A small thing that makes a big difference. I use this to create smooth, fluffy mashed potatoes and tender gnocchi dough. It gently breaks down the potato without overworking it—no gluey mash here.

Roasting Pan

Whether I'm slow-roasting a cut of meat or just catching drips under a cake, a good roasting pan comes in handy. I recommend one with a rack, which gives better airflow and more even browning.

Slotted Spoon

This is one of those unsung heroes. I use it constantly—for lifting fried foods, poached eggs, or blanched veggies out of hot liquid without bringing the liquid with them. It's simple, but essential.

Springform Cake Pans

I keep a few different sizes in my kitchen for baking everything from delicate sponge cakes to dense tortes. Springform pans are especially useful for desserts like cheesecakes and flans—anything that needs a gentle touch when unmolding.

Wire Cooking Racks

These are more versatile than they look. I use them for cooling baked goods, draining fried foods, and even building a DIY smoker setup (check out the Black Tea-Smoked Duck on page 186). They're all about air circulation, which means better texture every time.

A NOTE ABOUT FOOD & BEVERAGE PAIRINGS

Understanding the basics of food and beverage pairings is essential to elevating the dining experience. As a chef, I approach pairing much like I approach creating a dish—with balance, harmony, and a deep respect for how flavors interact. Whether you're serving a weeknight dinner or hosting a celebration, knowing how to pair your food with wine, champagne, beer or even cocktails can bring out the best in every bite and sip.

At the core of any good pairing is the idea of complementing or contrasting flavors. In wine, we often talk about acidity, tannins, body, sweetness, and alcohol level. A crisp Sauvignon Blanc with high acidity works wonders with dishes that have fresh herbs or citrus—think grilled shrimp with lemon or a goat cheese salad. The wine cuts through fat and refreshes the palate, making each bite feel like the first. On the other hand, a full-bodied Cabernet Sauvignon with firm tannins pairs beautifully with rich, fatty meats like ribeye or lamb. The tannins bind with the protein and fat, softening the wine and enhancing the meat's flavor.

Champagne and sparkling wines are more versatile than many people realize. Their acidity and bubbles make them a natural partner for salty or fried foods—oysters, fried chicken, and even potato chips all shine next to a glass of Brut Champagne. The effervescence also cleanses the palate between bites, making it ideal for multi-course meals.

Beer can also offer a wide spectrum of flavors, from crisp lagers to robust stouts. A hoppy IPA can stand up to spicy food—its bitterness balancing out the heat in dishes like spicy Korean wings or Indian curries. A malty porter, on the other hand, with its notes of coffee and chocolate, pairs beautifully with roasted meats or rich desserts like flourless chocolate cake.

Cocktails, while more complex, offer incredible pairing opportunities when treated like another ingredient in the dish. A gin and tonic with cucumber and mint can echo the freshness of a summer salad or ceviche. A bourbon old fashioned, with its smoky-sweet profile, pairs well with grilled meats or dishes with caramelized flavors, like roasted root vegetables or glazed pork belly.

When pairing beverages with food, consider the intensity of both. A delicate poached fish can be overwhelmed by a bold red wine, just as a light salad might get lost next to a boozy cocktail. Think about balance: sweet with spicy, acidic with fatty, bitter with umami. The goal is not to have one element dominate, but to create a dialogue between the food and the drink.

In my recipes, you'll often see beverage suggestions. These aren't random—they're crafted to complement the flavors and textures in the dish, enhancing the overall experience. Once you understand a few guiding principles of pairing, you'll find it easier to create your own matches and enjoy your meals on a whole new level. After all, food and drink are meant to be enjoyed together—and when done right, they're far greater than the sum of their parts.

WHAT'S COOKING IN OUR KITCHEN

In this cookbook, I've chosen to organize the chapters by primary ingredients rather than by course or cuisine. Each chapter is centered around one key ingredient—whether it's fruit, vegetables, pastas, or shellfish—and brings together a variety of recipes that showcase its versatility. This ingredient-driven structure is intentional and designed to make it easier for you to navigate the book and find exactly what you're looking for.

We've all opened the fridge, found a beautiful bunch of asparagus or a few pieces of salmon, and thought, *What can I make with this?* With this layout, you can simply flip to the ingredient you have on hand and browse a curated collection of recipes built around it. It's practical, intuitive, and reflects how most of us cook at home—starting with what we already have or what's in season.

You'll find a range of dishes in each chapter that span cooking styles, cultures, and flavor profiles, often with suggested beverage pairings to round out the experience.

This format also encourages creativity. Seeing how one ingredient can be used in multiple ways—grilled, roasted, raw, or braised—inspires confidence and helps build a deeper understanding of flavor and technique.

Ultimately, this ingredient-based approach puts the focus on what matters most: the food itself. This book is meant to be a tool, not just a collection of recipes. My hope is that it becomes a trusted companion in your kitchen, one you can turn to again and again for inspiration, clarity, and delicious results.

SPECIALTY COCKTAILS

Behind the bar at Salum, crafting cocktails is as much about storytelling as it is about flavor. These drinks bring together the vibrant spirit of Latin America with a global twist—just like the food we serve. Bright citrus, lush tropical fruit, and a whisper of smoky mezcal or smooth tequila set a mood that's equal parts celebration and siesta. Designed to spark your palate and your party, these cocktails are perfect whether you're gathered on a breezy patio or just daydreaming of one. From the zesty zing of a Cantarito to the blushing fizz of prosecco and limoncello, each sip is a mini vacation in a glass. So, shake, stir, and rim those glasses with salt or a sprinkle of Tajin—because I believe life's always better with a bold pour and a citrus twist.

Crazy World Cantarito

This bright, citrusy cocktail is our playful spin on the classic Cantarito—a beloved Mexican street drink known for its vibrant flavor and festive presentation. With bold splashes of lime and orange juice, a whisper of agave, and a fizzy pink grapefruit topper, this drink delivers sunshine in every sip. Don't forget the Tajin-dusted fruit garnish—it's the spicy-sweet kiss that brings it all home.

Makes 1 cocktail

1½ ounces Loca Loka Reposado Tequila
½ ounce fresh lime juice
1 ounce fresh orange juice
½ ounce agave nectar
3 ounces sparkling pink grapefruit soda
Garnish: Julienned sliced fruit, Tajin sprinkle

Add the tequila, lime and orange juices, agave nectar, and grapefruit soda to a ceramic mug filled with ice. Stir well, garnish, and serve.

Crazy World Cantarito (bottom right),
Crimson Cloud (top left)

Crimson Cloud

Bright, breezy, and just a little bit flirty, this cocktail is as eye-catching as it is refreshing. Muddled raspberries bring a pop of tart-sweet flavor and that signature blush hue, while lime and simple syrup keep things crisp and balanced. Stolichnaya Elit Vodka lends a silky, ultra-clean finish that lets the fruit shine—making this a lighthearted sip with just enough edge, perfect for sunset soirées or a relaxed night in.

Makes 1 cocktail

1½ ounces Stolichnaya Elit Vodka
½ ounce fresh lime juice
1 ounce simple syrup
5 fresh raspberries
Garnish: Fresh raspberry and mint sprig skewer

Add the vodka, lime juice, simple syrup, and raspberries to a cocktail shaker. Add some ice to the shaker, shake vigorously 15 to 20 times, then strain into a coupe or martini glass. Garnish and serve.

Desert Rose

As vibrant as a desert bloom after a summer rain, this cocktail is a stunner from first glance to final sip. Loca Loka Blanco Tequila brings its crisp, vegetal notes to the party, while a splash of hibiscus rose syrup adds a floral twist and that unmistakable fuchsia hue. Balanced with fresh lime and a touch of agave, it's bright, tart, and totally refreshing. Rimmed in pink Himalayan salt and crowned with a hibiscus flower, the Desert Rose is equal parts sultry and celebratory—an ode to bold flavors and warm summer nights.

Makes 1 cocktail

1½ ounces Loca Loka Blanco Tequila
¼ ounce hibiscus rose syrup
¾ ounce fresh lime juice
½ ounce agave nectar
Garnish: Hibiscus flower
Rim: lime wedge, Pink Himalayan salt

Run a fresh lime wedge around half the rim of a margarita or large coupe glass. Then roll the moistened rim in Pink Himalayan salt. Fill with ice and set the glass aside.

Add the tequila, syrup, lime juice, and agave nectar to a cocktail shaker. Add some ice to the shaker, shake vigorously 10 to 15 times, then strain into the prepared glass. Garnish and serve.

Juliette's Daydream

Light and lovely, this cocktail is what you sip when the sun is shining, and your only plan is to savor the moment. With fragrant Juliette Liqueur and citrusy limoncello, this sparkling spritz is bursting with floral and fruit notes—like a Mediterranean garden in full bloom. Topped with prosecco and garnished with juicy peach slices, it's fresh, fizzy, and fanciful.

Makes 1 cocktail

3/4 ounce Juliette Liqueur
3/4 ounce limoncello
4 ounces prosecco
Garnish: Peach slices

Add the liqueur, limoncello, and prosecco to a wine glass filled with ice. Stir, garnish, and serve.

Desert Rose (left)

Let Them Drink Cake

Get ready to party with this playful cocktail that's pure indulgence in a glass. Let Them Drink Cake takes classic Southern flavors—peach whiskey and rich rum cream—and swirls them together with a dash of black walnut bitters for a little extra depth. Topped off with Mardi Gras sprinkles or a mini cake garnish, this drink is a celebration of dessert, spirits, and good times.

Makes 1 cocktail

1 ounce Hardhide Peach Whiskey
1 ounce King Cake Rum Cream
1 dash black walnut bitters, optional
Garnish: Mardi Gras sprinkles or mini cake

Add the whiskey, rum cream, and bitters, if using, to a mixing glass filled with ice. Stir well until chilled. Strain into a double old fashioned glass filled with one large ice cube or sphere. Garnish and serve.

Let Them Drink Cake (bottom right)

CHEESE

Cheese has a way of stealing the spotlight, and in these recipes, it takes center stage. Rooted in the spirited, melting-pot cuisine of Texas, I'm naturally drawn to cheeses with a Mexican twist: spicy chorizo crumbles, smoky heat, and fresh herbs layered over gooey, melty goodness. In this chapter, you'll find recipes that lean into cheese's natural magic—whether it's the stretchy pull of mozzarella, the bold punch of blue, or the tangy creaminess of goat cheese. I love pairing these cheeses with flavors that complement and elevate—smoky prosciutto, toasted Marcona almonds, honey-drizzled fruit, and more. From apps to sweets, these cheese-forward dishes are made for gathering, sharing, and savoring slowly, with wine in hand and good company nearby. They're rich without being fussy, indulgent without apology—perfect for a long afternoon graze or a dinner party that lingers well into the evening.

Blue Cheese–Filled Figs Wrapped in Crispy Prosciutto

with Balsamic-Honey Glaze

This gorgeous appetizer is a real winner. The figs provide a juicy, tender bite, with their natural sweetness enhancing the rich, tangy blue cheese nestled inside. The prosciutto, when crisped up in the pan, adds a savory saltiness that contrasts beautifully with the softness of the figs and the creaminess of the cheese. To finish, a drizzle of honey-kissed balsamic glaze, with its sweet and tangy notes, ties everything together, to ensure each bite boasts a beautiful burst of flavor.

Serves 6 to 8

Balsamic-Honey Glaze

Makes ¼ cup

4 tablespoons balsamic vinegar
2 tablespoons honey
12 fresh figs
¾ cup crumbled blue cheese
12 slices prosciutto
1 tablespoon extra-virgin olive oil
½ teaspoon fresh cracked black pepper

To make the Balsamic-Honey Glaze: Add the balsamic vinegar and honey to a small saucepan. Bring to a simmer over medium heat and cook for about 5 to 7 minutes, until the mixture thickens slightly. Note: Be sure to stir occasionally and keep an eye on it to avoid burning. The glaze should be syrupy but not overly thick. Reserve at room temperature until ready to use.

Slice the figs in half and remove the stems. Use a small spoon to gently scoop out a little of the center to make room for the blue cheese stuffing. Add the blue cheese—about 1 teaspoon per fig half—to stuff the hollowed-out center of each fig. Take 1 slice of prosciutto and wrap it around each stuffed fig, covering it as best as you can. Note: The prosciutto will help to secure the cheese inside, so be sure to wrap it as best you can.

Heat the olive oil in a large skillet over medium heat. Once the oil is shimmering, add the wrapped figs in batches, being careful not to crowd the pan. Cook the figs for about 2 to 3 minutes on each side, or until the prosciutto is crispy and golden brown, and the cheese inside starts to soften.

Once all the figs are cooked, transfer them to a serving platter. Drizzle with the Balsamic-Honey Glaze and finish with the black pepper. Serve warm.

BEVERAGE SUGGESTION

I like to pair this dish with a glass of chilled amontillado sherry like Lustau. The sweetness of the figs, richness of the cheese, and salty prosciutto will complement the nutty and tobacco flavors of the sherry.

Crispy Fried Mozzarella & Ham Toasts

with Creamy Béchamel Sauce

Mozzarella in Carrozza is a classic Italian appetizer consisting of mozzarella cheese sandwiched between slices of bread, and coated in egg and breadcrumbs, then fried to golden perfection. The crispy exterior contrasts beautifully with the warm, gooey melty cheese inside, making it a comforting and indulgent starter. As an appetizer, it sets the stage for a meal by offering a rich, satisfying bite without being overly heavy. Chef's tip: You can accompany this with a tomato ragout for dipping or substitute the ham for anchovies for a briny note.

Serves 4

Béchamel Sauce

Makes about ½ cup

1 tablespoon unsalted butter
3 teaspoons all-purpose flour
½ cup whole milk
⅛ teaspoon kosher salt

Fried Mozzarella & Ham Toasts

½ cup all-purpose flour
¼ teaspoon kosher salt, divided
⅛ teaspoon fresh cracked black pepper
2 large eggs
1 tablespoon whole milk
½ cup panko-style breadcrumbs

BEVERAGE SUGGESTION

Drink a nice glass of chilled prosecco to accompany the toasts. Prosecco is vibrant yet approachable, elegant yet easy-drinking—a perfect companion to salty snacks, creamy cheeses, and moments worth toasting.

4 slices thick white sandwich bread, crust removed
4 deli-style mozzarella slices
2 thin-cut ham slices
½ cup light olive oil, divided
Micro flowers, for garnish, optional

To make the Béchamel Sauce: Add the butter to a medium-sized saucepan over medium heat. When the butter is melted, whisk in the flour and cook for several minutes to create a roux. Add the milk, stirring slowly, and let the sauce begin to thicken, then add the salt. Keep stirring until sauce is thickened and smooth; it should coat the back of a spoon. Set aside to cool for a few minutes before using. Any leftover béchamel can be stored in an airtight container in the refrigerator for 3 to 5 days.

For the toast prep, begin by setting up three dredging stations: First, add the flour to a plate and season lightly with ⅛ teaspoon of the salt and all the pepper, mixing to combine. To make the dipping mixture, beat the eggs, milk, and the remaining ⅛ teaspoon salt together in a pie tin or other flat container with sides. Finally, add the breadcrumbs to the third plate.

To assemble, spread about 1 tablespoon of the béchamel sauce on each slice of the bread, then lay down 2 slices of mozzarella and 1 slice of ham, topping with another piece of bread to create a sandwich, and smooshing it down lightly to seal the edges. Place the bread first in the flour, turning to coat, then in the egg dipping mixture, and finally in the breadcrumbs, coating all sides well. Repeat the process to create a second sandwich. Add 2 tablespoons of oil to a medium-sized skillet over medium-high heat. When the oil is shimmering, add one sandwich and fry. When the underside is nicely browned, flip over. Remove when both sides are nicely browned and the cheese is melted. Repeat with the remaining sandwiches. To serve, cut each sandwich in half and garnish with micro flowers, if using.

Micro Flowers & Micro Greens

As a chef, I've always been inspired by the vibrance and versatility that micro flowers and micro greens bring to a plate. These delicate ingredients aren't just garnish—they're bursts of flavor, color, and texture that transform food into art. That's why you'll find them in many of my dishes.

Micro flowers, with their brilliant hues and subtle flavors, such as fennel flowers, marigold, and violets, add an element of surprise and playfulness. Meanwhile, micro greens also contribute fresh intensity. Micro celery, cilantro, Hearts on Fire, Red Shiso, and Intensity Mix, for example, each offering a concentrated essence of the plant. Together, they create a symphony of taste and visual delight.

What excites me most is the sheer abundance and endless variety. With dozens of flowers and greens to choose from, the combinations are virtually limitless. A single plate can bloom with color, height, and freshness—whether it's a vibrant garnish on an entrée, a floral lift to a salad, or a delicate finish to a cocktail or dessert.

Beyond their beauty, micro flowers and greens allow chefs to layer flavor in subtle, unexpected ways while heightening presentation. They invite diners to pause, admire, and savor. For me, these ingredients are pure joy—tiny, living reminders that food is meant to be vibrant, fun, and endlessly creative.

Arugula Blossoms

Buls Blood

Fennel Flowers

Marigolds

Violas

Micro Chef's Blend

Micro Cilantro

Micro Hearts on Fire

Micro Celery

Micro Intensity Mix

Micro Red Shiso

Micro Flowers

Micro Violets

Fragrant Malbec-Poached Pears

with Cabrales Cheese & Toasted Marcona Almond Purée

Poached pears in red wine are a true delicacy, offering a perfect balance of sweetness and spice, infused with the rich, velvety depth of the wine. When complemented by a creamy, tangy blue cheese filling—crafted from the likes of Cabrales or any other robust variety—the contrast between the soft, juicy pear and the bold, salty cheese is simply divine. To elevate the experience, a sprinkle of crunchy Marcona almonds adds a delightful nutty texture—serve these as an appetizer, on top of a salad, or as a stand-alone dessert; they are sublime no matter how you choose to serve them.

Serves 4

4 slightly underripe Bosc pears
1 cup water
1 bottle Malbec wine
1 cup sugar
2 cinnamon sticks
2 star anise
2 whole cloves
4 tablespoons crumbled Cabrales or other strong blue cheese
½ cup toasted Marcona almonds
Micro flowers, for garnish, optional

Peel the pears and remove the cores using a melon baller or corer. Chef's tip: Insert the tool into the bottom of the pear and twist to remove the core, creating a pocket in the middle, but keeping the stem end intact. Set the pears aside.

Add the water, wine, sugar, cinnamon sticks, star anise, and cloves to a large stock-pot over medium-high heat. Bring to a boil. Add the pears and poach for 25 minutes

Meet Cabrales

Spain's Funky Blue Powerhouse

Bold, briny, and unapologetically intense, Cabrales is a Spanish blue cheese that doesn't whisper—it shouts. Produced in the Asturias region of northern Spain, this cow's milk cheese (sometimes blended with goat or sheep's milk) is aged in natural limestone caves, where the cool, damp air helps the signature blue-green veins flourish. Cabrales has a dense, crumbly texture and a fiery sharpness that lingers on the palate. It's not for the faint of heart—but it is a dream when paired with something sweet. That's why it's perfect in this dish: the warm spice of poached pears and the nutty creaminess of Marcona almonds bring out its more nuanced side. Serving tip: Let Cabrales come to room temperature before using. It mellows slightly and becomes beautifully spreadable—the ideal consistency for the purée found here, or for serving on a bold cheese board.

or until tender, keeping the liquid at a rolling simmer. Remove the pears and continue to boil the poaching liquid for an additional 45 minutes, or until the mixture is reduced by half. Set aside and reserve.

Add the Cabrales or blue cheese and toasted almonds to a food processor and purée, pulsing until the cheese is smooth, but some small pieces of the almonds remain intact. Place the mixture in a pastry bag fitted with a piping tip. Carefully pipe the purée into each pear, filling the pocket completely.

To finish, arrange a poached pear on each plate and drizzle with the reduced poaching liquid, serving extra alongside, as desired. Garnish with micro flowers, if using, and serve.

Summer Berry, Mascarpone & Goat Cheese Tarts

with Basil-Infused Honey Drizzle

These petite tarts are a delightful fusion of flavors, combining the richness of goat cheese and mascarpone with the freshness of ripe berries. The filling is smooth and creamy, nestled in a crisp, buttery tart shell. To elevate the experience, a drizzle of honey infused with basil essential oil adds an aromatic and slightly herbal note, perfectly complementing the sweetness of the berries. These tarts are a unique and elegant dessert, perfect for special occasions, or a refined treat any time of year, thanks to the year-round availability of fresh berries. For the basil essential oil, you can find this in grocery or retail stores in the health foods section, or it is readily available online.

Serves 6

Basil-Infused Honey

Makes 1 cup

1 cup honey

¼ teaspoon basil essential oil

Summer Berry, Mascarpone & Goat Cheese Tarts

TART SHELLS

6 tablespoons room temperature unsalted butter

½ cup confectioners' sugar

2 large egg yolks

1 beaten whole egg

1 teaspoon pure vanilla extract

2 cups all-purpose flour

1 beaten egg white

BEVERAGE SUGGESTION

Enjoy a fine glass of white port such as Ramos Pinto Lagrima and you will be in heaven. White Port is a lesser-known gem in the world of fortified wines—elegant, slightly sweet, and refreshingly complex.

FILLING & TOPPING

1 cup goat cheese
½ cup mascarpone or cream cheese
1 cup heavy cream
2 to 3 cups fresh mixed strawberries, raspberries, blackberries, and blueberries
Micro basil, for garnish, optional

To make the Basil-Infused Honey: Add the honey to a small bowl. Using the pipette dropper that comes with the oil, add the basil essential oil into the honey one drop at time, mixing well to incorporate after each drop. Chef's tip: The ¼ teaspoon should take about 8 drops total. Reserve at room temperature until ready for use. Leftovers can be stored in an airtight container at room temperature for 2 to 3 weeks.

Preheat the oven to 350°F.

To prepare the tart dough, add the butter and confectioners' sugar to the bowl of an electric mixer fitted with a paddle attachment. Cream together on medium speed until the mixture is light and fluffy, about 2 to 3 minutes.

With the mixer running at medium, add in the egg yolks, then the beaten whole egg and vanilla, mixing well between each addition. Add the flour and mix until just combined. The dough should be soft, but not sticky, and stick together when pressed between two fingers. Wrap the dough in plastic wrap, form it into a disc shape, and chill in the refrigerator for at least 2 hours or overnight.

Note: You will need six 4-inch-wide round mini tart pans for this recipe. Remove the dough from the refrigerator and unwrap. Divide the dough into 6 equal balls. Using a rolling pin, roll out each ball on a large, floured surface into a rough circular shape until the dough is about ¼-inch-thick. Flip them over once or twice as you roll and add more flour to the surface if the dough gets too tacky. Drape each of the rounds into a tart pan and press the dough down evenly across the bottom and up the sides of the pan. Trim any excess dough from the tops.

Line the tarts with parchment paper and fill with pie weights or dried beans. Place all 6 tarts on a large, lightly colored baking sheet and bake in the oven for 20 minutes, until golden brown. Remove and allow the tart shells to cool for about 5 minutes. While still warm, remove the weights and parchment paper and brush the shells lightly with the beaten egg white using a pastry brush. Tip: Take care not to use too much and to only brush the inside of the shells. Let the tart shells cool to room temperature before adding filling. Note: Tart shells can be prepared up to 1 day in advance.

To prepare the filling, add the goat cheese, mascarpone, and heavy cream to a medium size bowl. Mix using a non-stick spatula until smooth and creamy. Place the filling in a pastry bag outfitted with a large piping tip.

To assemble, pipe about ½ cup of the filling into each tart shell until it is even with the top of the crust. Drizzle the Basil-Infused Honey over the tarts, 1 tablespoon per tart, and then decorate each with fresh berries and micro basil, if using. Serve immediately, or refrigerate until ready to serve, up to 1 day in advance.

Note: This recipe can be adapted to suit whichever size tart pan you might have; the portions here also work well in two 9-inch-wide round tart pans. For two tarts, use the same method for baking, but check the shells at 20 minutes and continue baking for an additional 3 to 5 minutes, if necessary, to ensure doneness.

Goat Cheese

Tart, Tangy,
& Totally Dessert Worthy

While goat cheese is most often associated with savory dishes—like salads, flatbreads, and cheese boards—it has a secret superpower: it's dreamy in desserts. Its creamy texture and signature tang add a sophisticated twist to sweet recipes, creating a beautiful contrast to sugary ingredients like fruit, chocolate, or honey. In these Summer Berry Tarts, goat cheese partners with mascarpone and cream to create a filling that's rich, smooth, and just slightly tart—providing the perfect counterpoint to sweet, ripe berries and floral basil-infused honey. The result is balanced, elegant, and anything but ordinary. Looking to experiment further? Goat cheese pairs beautifully with roasted figs, dark chocolate, poached pears, or even lemon curd. Use it in cheesecake, swirl it into brownies, or blend it into frostings for an unexpected—and wildly delicious—upgrade.

Triple-Cheese Mexican Fundido

with Spicy Chorizo Crumbles

Our spin on queso fundido, this dish is rich and flavorful, combining three different melted cheeses with the bold, spicy kick of sausage. The savory, slightly smoky chorizo adds a perfect contrast to the creamy, gooey cheese, creating a mouthwatering combination. Queso fundido is a staple in taquerías across Mexico as it is not only delicious, but also versatile—it can be served as a standalone dip with warm tortillas, as seen here, or enjoyed drizzled over tacos, nachos, and more. The irresistible blend of textures and flavors make it a favorite for sharing.

Serves 6

1 tablespoon vegetable oil
5 ounces Mexican chorizo, casings removed
1 cup grated Oaxaca cheese
1 cup grated Asadero cheese
½ cup grated Mexican Manchego cheese
Salsa, for serving
Flour or corn tortillas, for serving
Micro cilantro, for garnish, optional

Preheat the oven to 350°F.

Add the vegetable oil to a medium-size skillet over medium-high heat. When the oil is shimmering, add the chorizo and cook for 6 to 7 minutes, or until the chorizo is browned and cooked through, stirring frequently and breaking the meat into small pieces. Move the cooked chorizo to a paper towel–lined plate. Allow to cool for a few minutes.

Queso Fundido

A Northern Mexican Classic

Queso fundido—which literally means "melted cheese"—is Mexico's answer to fondue, and it's every bit as crave-worthy. Rooted in Northern Mexican and Tex-Mex traditions, this bubbling skillet of gooey cheese often stars at casual family dinners, fiestas, or late-night gatherings. Originally inspired by the rustic cooking of Northern ranchers and miners, queso fundido was designed to be hearty, simple, and deeply satisfying. It's traditionally made with Oaxaca, Asadero, or Chihuahua cheese—melty varieties that stretch and pull with every bite. Unlike American-style queso dip, queso fundido isn't saucy. Served sizzling straight from the oven or comal, it's stringy and dense—because in the world of queso fundido, the longer the cheese pull, the louder the applause.

Place the chorizo in an ovenproof dish, setting aside 2 tablespoons for garnish later. Sprinkle the grated cheeses over the chorizo and bake for 10 to 12 minutes, or until the cheese is melted and bubbling. Note: Overcooking the fondue will result in a chewy texture, so be sure to keep an eye on the oven as it cooks.

Remove from the oven and place the fondue onto a heat-resistant surface. Garnish with the reserved chorizo and micro cilantro, if using. Serve immediately with salsa and flour or corn tortillas alongside.

Beverage Suggestion

I find the ideal pairing for queso fundido is a classic margarita. The acidity from the lime juice and the bite of tequila complement the richness of the cheese. A spicy margarita (with jalapeño or chili salt) will match any heat in the queso.

Mexican Oaxaca Cheese

FRUIT

Fruit doesn't just belong in dessert—and in my kitchen, it's often the unexpected star of savory dishes. Bright, juicy, and sometimes surprising, fruit brings a welcome burst of contrast to smoky bacon, creamy avocado, aged cheese, and fragrant herbs. Drawing inspiration from my favorite Latin flavors, where fruit is celebrated boldly, these recipes highlight the beauty of sweet and heat, acid and earth, in perfect harmony. For me, fruit isn't just a garnish; it's the heart of the dish—folded into vibrant salads, roasted into savory stuffings, or grilled until caramelized and sweet. From the crisp snap of green papaya to the lush ripeness of summer peaches, these plates are about balance and brightness—designed to awaken your palate and keep every bite fresh, vibrant, and anything but ordinary.

Date, Orange & Pistachio Salad

with Citrus-Honey Balsamic Vinaigrette

This fresh and vibrant salad combines the sweetness of dates and oranges with the crunch of pistachios, creating a bright balance of textures and tastes. The mixed greens also provide a mild peppery bite, especially if you're using arugula or watercress, while the red onion introduces a light sharpness that cuts through the richness of the dates and nuts. The mint offers a refreshing herbal note, giving the salad a bright and cool finish. The dressing—made from orange juice, honey, balsamic vinegar, and olive oil—adds a tangy-sweet depth, with a touch of acidity from the vinegar that ties everything together beautifully. It's an excellent side dish or light lunch, and it pairs beautifully with grilled meats or seafood.

Serves 4

Citrus-Honey Balsamic Vinaigrette

Makes ½ cup

2 tablespoons olive oil
1 tablespoon honey or maple syrup
1 tablespoon fresh squeezed orange juice
1 teaspoon balsamic vinegar
¼ teaspoon kosher salt
¼ teaspoon fresh cracked black pepper

Date, Orange & Pistachio Salad

6 to 8 pitted and sliced Medjool dates
2 large peeled and segmented oranges
1 small red onion, peeled and thinly sliced
4 cups mixed greens, such as arugula, spinach, or watercress

½ cup roasted, roughly chopped pistachios
¼ cup fresh torn mint leaves

To make the Citrus-Honey Balsamic Vinaigrette: Add the olive oil, honey or maple syrup, orange juice, balsamic vinegar, salt, and pepper to a small bowl. Whisk until well combined and reserve until ready to use. The vinaigrette can be prepped ahead and stored in an airtight container on the counter for several hours, or in the refrigerator for up to 2 to 3 days. Bring vinaigrette to room temperature and stir well before using.

Add the sliced dates, orange segments, red onions, and mixed greens to a large mixing bowl. Toss lightly to combine. Add in the chopped pistachios and fresh mint leaves. Drizzle the Citrus-Honey Balsamic Vinaigrette over the salad and gently toss to combine all the ingredients, ensuring everything is coated evenly. Plate the salad and serve immediately, garnishing with a few extra pistachios and mint leaves, if desired.

Grilled Summer Peach Salad

with Guajillo Buttermilk Dressing & Candied Pepitas

This salad sings of summer, featuring juicy grilled peaches and tender lettuce greens. A topping of roasted pepitas provides both a delightful crunch and a touch of sweetness courtesy of their caramelized coating. The guajillo buttermilk dressing brings a creamy, slightly spicy flavor, enhancing the dish with its smoky depth. Fresh herbs like mint, cilantro, and parsley help finish this stunning dish. Serve it alongside a charred steak or pork chop, and it is summer at its finest.

Serves 6

Candied Pepitas

Makes 1½ cups

1½ cups raw pepita (pumpkin) seeds
½ cup packed dark brown sugar
½ teaspoon kosher salt
1 large egg white
1 teaspoon smoked paprika

Guajillo Buttermilk Dressing

Makes 2 cups

2 dried guajillo chile peppers
1½ cups buttermilk
2 teaspoons rice wine vinegar
½ cup extra-virgin olive oil
¼ teaspoon kosher salt, more to taste
¼ teaspoon fresh cracked black pepper, more to taste

Grilled Peach Salad

3 ripe, but still firm, peaches
¼ teaspoon kosher salt
¼ teaspoon fresh cracked black pepper
2 tablespoons extra-virgin olive oil, plus more for brushing
1 head red-leaf lettuce, such as Lollo Rosso
1 cup fresh herbs, such as a combination of chopped fresh mint, cilantro and parsley leaves, plus chives
Micro flowers, for garnish, optional

To make the Candied Pepitas: Preheat the oven to 350°F. Toss the pepita seeds with the brown sugar, salt, egg white, and smoked paprika in a mixing bowl. Add them to a sheet pan and roast in the preheated oven for about 15 minutes, or until they are lightly brown and crisp, and the sugar is caramelized. Note: Watch closely during the last 5 minutes of cooking to ensure the sugar doesn't burn. Remove and allow to cool to room temperature before using.

To prepare the Guajillo Buttermilk Dressing: Remove any seeds from the dried guajillo peppers. Add a few cups of water to a pot over medium heat and bring to a simmer. Once simmering, turn off the heat and add the peppers, allowing them to rehydrate in the water for about 5 minutes. Drain the water, and allow the peppers to cool to room temperature, about 10 minutes. Add the rehydrated peppers to a high-powered blender or a food processor fitted with a blade attachment, then add a few teaspoons of water. Purée until smooth, then mix in the buttermilk, rice wine vinegar, olive oil, salt, and pepper. Taste for seasoning, and add more salt and pepper, as needed. Reserve in the refrigerator until ready for use. The dressing can also be prepared ahead and stored in an airtight container in the refrigerator for 3 to 5 days.

To finish the dish, slice the peaches into 6 wedges each. Season with the salt and pepper and drizzle with the olive oil.

Caramelized & Charred

Grilling Fruit for Big Flavor

High-heat grilling transforms fruit like peaches, nectarines, and plums into smoky-sweet wonders. The natural sugars caramelize, creating a luscious, jammy texture with charred edges that add a whisper of bitterness—just enough to make things interesting. To grill, simply follow the same method as outlined in the Grilled Peaches recipe: slice firm, ripe fruit in half, brush lightly with oil and season with salt and pepper, and cook cut-side down on a hot grill for 2 to 4 minutes on each side, until grill marks appear. In addition to the stone fruit, I also love grilling citrus like lemons, oranges, and limes—the heat punches up their natural zesty flavors. Try squeezing grilled lime wedges over fish tacos, or whisk grilled orange juice into your favorite vinaigrette, for a fresh spin.

Preheat a grill or grill pan to medium heat and lightly brush the grates with olive oil to avoid sticking. Add the peach slices and grill on both sides for about 2 to 4 minutes on each, until they develop nice grill marks, but don't overcook—leave them firm. Remove and allow to cool for a few minutes.

Gently separate and clean the lettuce leaves, taking care not to bruise them. Arrange the lettuce on a large serving plate, add the fresh herbs over top, and place the grilled peaches all around. Drizzle with the Guajillo Buttermilk Dressing, sprinkle with Candied Pepitas and micro flowers, if using, and serve.

BEVERAGE SUGGESTION

A lightly chilled Viognier or off-dry Riesling like Selbach from Mosel pairs wonderfully with a grilled summer peach salad topped with guajillo buttermilk dressing and candied pepitas. The wine's stone fruit notes echo the sweetness of the peaches, while its acidity and gentle spice balance the smoky heat of the guajillo. Its smooth, slightly floral finish complements the creamy dressing and crunch of the candied pepitas.

Mayan Citrus Salad

with Jicama, Grapefruit & Lime

Bright, bold, and rooted in tradition, Xec is a classic Mayan salad that turns simple fruit into something unforgettable. Crisp matchsticks of jicama mingle with juicy segments of orange and mandarin, all tossed in a punchy mix of citrus juices and chiles. The result is a salad that's cooling and refreshing with just the right amount of heat. Chopped cilantro adds an herbaceous lift, while the blend of orange, lime, and grapefruit juice acts as both dressing and flavor amplifier. It's a vibrant side dish, snack, or palate cleanser that tastes like sunshine—and wakes up every bite.

Serves 4

1 medium jicama
4 small oranges
3 mandarins
⅓ cup chopped fresh cilantro leaves
¼ cup fresh squeezed orange juice
¼ cup lime juice
¼ cup grapefruit juice
1 teaspoon ground piquín pepper or Tajín seasoning
¼ teaspoon kosher salt, more to taste
Micro cilantro, for garnish, optional

Peel and chop the jicama into thin strips or matchsticks. Peel the oranges and mandarins, then cut them into segments. Combine the jicama and oranges in a large bowl, along with the cilantro. Set aside.

Add the orange juice, lime juice, grapefruit juice, and piquín pepper or Tajin seasoning to a small bowl and mix to combine. Pour the dressing over the salad and toss gently. Season with the salt. Taste for seasoning, and add more salt, if desired. Transfer to a large serving platter, or individual salad plates, garnish with the mico greens, if using, and serve.

ORIGIN STORY

Xec's Mayan Roots

Xec is a traditional fruit salad from the Yucatán region of Mexico, often served during holidays or festive gatherings. The name comes from the Mayan word for "mix," and that's exactly what this dish is—a bright, refreshing medley of citrus fruits, jicama, and chili, perhaps either fiery piquín pepper or tangy Tajín for a fun, fruity twist. Popular during the Day of the Dead and other seasonal celebrations, Xec embodies the balance so central to Mayan cuisine: sweet, sour, salty, spicy, and fresh. While traditionally made with bitter oranges and ground piquín chile, modern variations often incorporate mandarins and grapefruit, for a fruitier twist. However it's made, Xec is a celebration of contrast and flavor, meant to awaken the palate.

Roasted Granny Smith Apples

with Turkey, Almond & Sage Stuffing over Garlic-Tomato Sofrito

This fruit-forward entrée boasts the perfect balance of sweet and savory, combining the tartness of Granny Smith apples with a flavorful ground turkey stuffing. The meat is sautéed with a mix of aromatic vegetables, smoked paprika, fresh herbs, and crunchy almonds, creating a hearty, yet healthy filling. The apples are carefully hollowed out and stuffed with this mixture, then roasted to perfection. Served over a bed of rich sofrito—a tomato-based sauce with garlic, onions, and herbs—this dish is aromatic and appealing, cozy and comforting; it's sure to be a return favorite.

Serves 6

Garlic-Tomato Sofrito

Makes about 2 cups

½ cup extra-virgin olive oil
8 cloves garlic, peeled and finely minced
4 cups finely chopped yellow or white onion
1 teaspoon fresh thyme leaves
1 teaspoon fresh rosemary leaves
1 dried bay leaf
1 (8-ounce) can tomato purée
½ teaspoon kosher salt, more to taste
¼ teaspoon fresh cracked black pepper, more to taste

Roasted Granny Smith Apples with Turkey, Almond & Sage Stuffing

6 Granny Smith apples
2 teaspoons extra-virgin olive oil
1 pound 90/10 ground turkey

½ cup finely chopped celery
½ cup peeled and finely chopped onion
1 teaspoon smoked paprika
2 cloves garlic, peeled and finely chopped
2 tablespoons finely chopped sage leaves
2 tablespoons finely chopped parsley leaves
½ cup chopped Marcona or regular almonds
¼ teaspoon kosher salt
¼ teaspoon fresh cracked black pepper
Micro Hearts on Fire, for garnish, optional

To prepare the Garlic-Tomato Sofrito: Add the olive oil to a medium saucepan over medium heat. Once the oil is shimmering, add the minced garlic and fry the garlic until browned, about 2 to 3 minutes. Add the onions, thyme, rosemary and bay leaf, and continue cooking until the onions are browned, an additional 3 to 4 minutes. Stir in about ¾ of the tomato purée and cook for 30 minutes. Add the rest of the tomatoes and cook for an additional 30 minutes, until the mixture is thick, and boasts a deep red color. Season with the salt and pepper, taste for seasoning, and add more, if desired. Keep warm until ready to serve.

Preheat the oven to 350°F.

Cut the tops from the apples using a sharp paring knife, then hollow out the apples using the same knife or an apple corer, creating a generous pocket for the stuffing and leaving the bottom of the apple intact. Reserve the apple flesh from inside the fruit, and finely mince. Set both the cored apples, and minced apple, aside.

Add the olive oil to a large sauté pan over medium heat. Once the oil is shimmering, add the ground turkey and brown for 5 to 6 minutes, breaking the meat into small pieces. Once the turkey is cooked through, add the reserved apple pieces, plus the celery, onion, paprika, garlic, sage and parsley. Mix well and then sauté until the vegetables are tender and the herbs are fragrant, about 5 minutes. Remove from the heat and stir in the almonds. Season with the salt and pepper, then allow the mixture to cool to room temperature, about 10 minutes.

Stuff the apples with the cooled turkey mixture, using about 2 to 3 tablespoons per apple, and loosely filling the hollowed-out pocket. Place in a large roasting dish and roast the apples in the oven for 40 minutes, or until the apples are tender and easily pierced with a fork. Remove from the oven.

To serve, place a helping of the Garlic-Tomato Sofrito on each plate, top with a stuffed apple, and garnish with micro greens, if using, and serve warm.

BEVERAGE SUGGESTION

This dish pairs beautifully with Sauvignon Blanc. Its bright acidity and citrus notes cut through the richness and echo the apples' tart-sweet profile. The wine's herbal undertones complement the sage, while its freshness keeps the dish light and balanced. I recommend Drylands Sauvignon Blanc from New Zealand or a more subtle Sancerre like Domaine Durand.

Watermelon, Red Onion, and Applewood Smoked Bacon Salad

with Balsamic Syrup & White Balsamic Vinaigrette

This salad is our warm-weather cure-all. It's bright and vibrant, combining sweet, juicy watermelon with peppery watercress, sharp red onion, and crispy bacon. Tossed in a bright white balsamic vinaigrette and drizzled with a rich balsamic syrup, it's a refreshing balance of sweet, savory, and tangy. It's best served very cold on a hot Texas afternoon.

Serves 6

White Balsamic Vinaigrette

Makes about ¾ cup

⅓ cup white balsamic vinegar
⅓ cup extra-virgin olive oil
1 tbsp Dijon mustard
¼ teaspoon kosher salt, more to taste
¼ teaspoon fresh cracked black pepper, more to taste

Balsamic Syrup

Makes 1½ cups

2 cups balsamic vinegar

Watermelon, Red Onion, and Applewood Smoked Bacon Salad

8 cups diced red seedless watermelon
6 small bunches watercress
1 red onion, peeled and thinly sliced

6 slices cooked and chopped applewood smoked bacon
¼ teaspoon kosher salt
¼ teaspoon fresh cracked black pepper
Micro marigold flowers, for garnish, optional

To make the White Balsamic Vinaigrette: Add the white balsamic vinegar, olive oil and Dijon mustard to a medium bowl and whisk well to combine. Note: You are looking for a smooth, nicely emulsified dressing. If necessary, you can add a few drops of water to help smooth it out as you whisk. Season with salt and pepper, adding more to taste, if desired. Reserve until ready for use. The vinaigrette can be prepared ahead of time and refrigerated for up to 1 week; bring to room temperature and mix well before using.

To prep the Balsamic Syrup: Add the balsamic vinegar to a non-reactive pan over medium-low heat. Bring to a very low simmer, then reduce the heat to low, and allow the vinegar to thicken to a syrup-like consistency, about 20 minutes. Set aside to cool and use at room temperature.

Add the watermelon, watercress, red onion, bacon, and the White Balsamic Vinaigrette to a mixing bowl and toss well to combine. To serve, portion the dressed salad onto chilled salad plates. Drizzle with the Balsamic Syrup and season with salt and pepper. Garnish with the micro flowers, if using, and serve cold.

EAST

PUBL

White Wine–Poached Quince

with Manchego Cheese, Heirloom Tomatoes & Piquillo Pepper Salad

Quince is a pome fruit, related to apples and pears, but with a distinctive flavor and texture. Here, we poach it in white wine along with honey and fragrant spices that infuse it with an aromatic flavor that pairs beautifully with the nutty, creamy Manchego cheese. Heirloom tomatoes add juiciness and acidity, while the piquillo peppers bring a mild, smoky sweetness. A drizzle of olive oil and red wine vinegar punches up the dish, all while still allowing the quinces natural flavors to shine.

Serves 4

4 ripe quinces
4 cups water
1 cup dry white wine
¼ cup honey
1 cinnamon stick
2 star anise
1 strip lemon peel
1 tablespoon sugar
1 cup thinly sliced Manchego cheese
3 to 4 heirloom tomatoes, sliced
½ cup jarred or roasted piquillo peppers, sliced
1 tablespoon extra-virgin olive oil
1 tablespoon red wine vinegar
¼ teaspoon kosher salt, more to taste
¼ teaspoon fresh cracked black pepper, more to taste
¼ cup fresh basil or mint leaves
Micro arugula, for garnish, optional

From Tough to Tender

Unlocking the Secrets of Quince

Quince is the quiet poet of the fruit bowl—pale, knobby, and unassuming on the outside, but full of deep, fragrant potential. Too astringent to eat raw, quince softens into velvet when cooked, releasing floral notes of apple, pear, and honey. In Spain, it's often simmered into membrillo, a firm fruit paste served with Manchego cheese. But poached in white wine, as in the recipe here, it becomes a delicate and aromatic counterpoint to savory elements like piquillo peppers or salty cheeses. Look for golden-yellow skin and a floral scent when ripe and treat it like a secret weapon in your fruit repertoire.

Peel and core the quince, then slice them into quarters. Add the water, white wine, honey, cinnamon stick, star anise, lemon peel, and sugar to a medium pot over medium heat. Bring the mixture to a gentle boil, then reduce the heat to low. Add the quince slices to the pan and let them simmer for about 45 minutes, or until they are tender and have taken on a rosy color. Once the quinces are poached, remove them from the liquid and set aside to cool. Note: You can keep the poaching liquid for later use, if desired, as a syrup or glaze.

On a large platter or individual plates, arrange the poached quince slices, then add the Manchego cheese slices, heirloom tomatoes, and piquillo peppers, layering them in an aesthetically pleasing manner on the platter, overlapping slightly. Drizzle the olive oil and red wine vinegar over the salad.

Sprinkle with the salt and pepper, adding more to taste. Scatter fresh basil or mint leaves on top of the salad, garnish with the micro greens, if using, and serve.

GREENS & VEGETABLES

Greens and vegetables are never just side notes in my kitchen—they're bold, vibrant, and full of personality. Drawing from my Lebanese roots and the Latin American and South Indian flavors I love, these recipes celebrate the incredible diversity of fresh produce and how different cultures bring it to life. Whether it's the smoky char on grilled romaine or the bright, tangy kick of chipotle-lime nopales, each dish layers spices, herbs, and textures to turn everyday veggies into unforgettable moments on the plate. Rooted in global traditions but with a unique twist, these bowls, soups, and salads show how vegetables can steal the show—whether cool and refreshing, warm and comforting, or smoky and complex. From a silky avocado gazpacho to the zing of South Indian Rasam, get ready to see these greens and veggies in a whole new light.

Chilled Avocado Gazpacho

with Shrimp, Heirloom Tomatoes & Fresh Corn in Pasilla Sauce

Creamy avocado takes center stage in this vibrant chilled soup, offering a lush, velvety base that's brightened by lime juice and other green vegetables like cucumber, celery, and tomatillo. But what truly sets this dish apart is its dramatic topping: sautéed shrimp tossed in a smoky pasilla chile sauce, layered with bursts of sweetness from heirloom tomatoes and fresh corn. The interplay of cool and spicy, creamy and crisp, makes this gazpacho a standout—summery and refreshing, but with enough depth to hold its own as a first course or light main. It's a bold, border-crossing twist on the Andalusian classic.

Serves 6

Chilled Avocado Gazpacho

½ cup diced bell peppers
2 husked tomatillos
½ cup torn, day-old bread chunks
2 cloves garlic, peeled and minced
4 cups fresh cilantro leaves
½ cucumber, peeled and chopped
3 avocados, peeled and pitted
2 celery stalks, chopped
½ cup lime juice
¼ cup extra-virgin olive oil
¼ teaspoon kosher salt, more to taste
¼ teaspoon fresh cracked black pepper, more to taste
Micro Bull's Blood, for garnish, optional

Shrimp, Heirloom Tomatoes & Fresh Corn in Pasilla Sauce

Makes about 6 cups

½ pound peeled and deveined shrimp
2 pasilla chiles, seeded, deveined, and finely chopped
2 cloves garlic, peeled and minced
1 cup baby heirloom or cherry tomatoes, halved
1 cup fresh-shucked corn kernels
⅛ teaspoon kosher salt, more to taste
⅛ teaspoon fresh cracked black pepper, more to taste

To prepare the Chilled Avocado Gazpacho: Add the bell peppers, tomatillos, bread, garlic, cilantro, cucumber, avocados, celery, lime juice, and olive oil to a high-powered blender or a food processor fitted with a blade attachment. Blend until smooth. Season with the salt and pepper, taste for seasoning, and add more, if desired. Chill the gazpacho in the refrigerator until ready to serve. Note: Try to chill your gazpacho for about 2 hours, or longer, to let the flavors meld.

To prepare the Shrimp, Heirloom Tomatoes & Fresh Corn in Pasilla Sauce: Add the shrimp to a medium sauté pan over medium heat. Add the chopped pasillas and garlic, and cook until the shrimp turn pink, about 2 to 3 minutes. Add the tomatoes and corn kernels and cook for 2 to 3 more minutes, until the corn is tender. Season with the salt and pepper, taste for seasoning, and add more, if desired. Serve immediately with the gazpacho. Leftovers can be stored for 1 to 3 days in an airtight container in the refrigerator.

To serve, place a small amount of the warm shrimp mixture in the center of each bowl. Pour the chilled gazpacho around the shrimp, garnish with the micro greens, if using, and serve.

A crisp Albariño like Coral do Mar from Rias Baixas, pairs beautifully with chilled avocado gazpacho topped with shrimp, heirloom tomatoes, and fresh corn in a pasilla sauce. The wine's bright acidity and citrusy minerality refresh the palate, while subtle salinity and stone fruit notes enhance the sweetness of the corn and balance the smoky pasilla.

Know Your Chiles

Pasilla, Poblano & More

Chiles bring more than just heat—they're the heart and soul of many of the soups, stews, sauces and salad vinaigrettes found in this book. From smoky-sweet to fiery and floral, each chile has its own personality.

Chilled Spanish Tomato Soup

with Chopped Egg & Cured Ham

Salmorejo is a rich, velvety cold tomato soup from Catalunya in Spain, typically enjoyed in the warmer months when tomatoes are at their peak. With its simple yet bold flavors of ripe tomatoes, garlic, and olive oil, it's a lovely choice for a light, satisfying appetizer or a refreshing afternoon snack. The topping of chopped egg and cured ham adds texture and flavor, another authentic Spanish touch.

Serves 6

3 slices white bread
1 cup water
1 pound ripe tomatoes, such as beefsteak or Roma, peeled and seeded
3 to 4 cloves garlic, peeled and chopped
½ teaspoon kosher salt, more to taste
½ teaspoon fresh cracked black pepper, more to taste
1 teaspoon sherry vinegar
¼ cup Spanish extra-virgin olive oil
1 hard-boiled egg, finely chopped
½ cup finely chopped Spanish cured ham, such as jamón Serrano or Iberico

Slice the bread into ½-inch-thick slices, then place the bread in a shallow bowl and pour the water over it. Let it soak for a few minutes.

Add the tomatoes and garlic to a high-powered blender or food processor fitted with a blade attachment. Process until chunky, then season with the salt and pepper. Add the sherry vinegar and olive oil and process until smooth.

Squeeze out the water from the bread and add it to the tomato mixture. Continue processing until the mixture becomes smooth and creamy. Taste for seasoning, and add more salt and pepper, if desired. Cover and chill in the refrigerator for at least 2 hours to allow the flavors to meld.

To serve, transfer to serving bowls and top each portion with finely chopped hard-boiled egg and Spanish cured ham. Serve chilled.

BEVERAGE SUGGESTION

Salmorejo, with its rich, creamy texture and bright tomato flavor, pairs wonderfully with a crisp, refreshing white wine like Verdejo or a dry Albariño. The wine's acidity cuts through the richness of the soup, while the soup complements the wine's fresh, herbal notes.

Lebanese-Inspired Chickpea & Yogurt Soup

with Chicken, Chili & Lemon

This soup draws inspiration from the comforting, flavorful broths found in Lebanese cuisine, where yogurt often plays a key role in creating rich, creamy soups with a subtle tang. The use of chickpeas adds an earthy element, while the chili flakes introduce a mild heat, which is characteristic of many Middle Eastern dishes. The addition of chicken also gives the soup a hearty, satisfying texture. The dish blends the richness of the yogurt with the warmth of garlic, the brightness of lemon, and the gentle heat of chili flakes, creating a perfect balance of refreshing flavors.

Serves 6

1½ tablespoons unsalted butter
2 tablespoons extra-virgin olive oil
1 leek, trimmed and sliced
2 cloves garlic, peeled and crushed
1 dried bay leaf
5 cups chicken stock
1½ pounds boneless, skinless chicken breasts
1 teaspoon cornstarch
⅔ cup plain natural yogurt
1 (7-ounce) can chickpeas, drained and rinsed
¼ teaspoon crushed red pepper flakes
Juice of 1 lemon
¼ teaspoon kosher salt, more to taste
¼ teaspoon fresh cracked black pepper, more to taste
2 tablespoons chopped fresh cilantro leaves

1/8 teaspoon ground paprika
Micro celery leaves, for garnish, optional

Melt the butter with the olive oil in in a large saucepan over low heat. Add the sliced leek and cook for 8 to 10 minutes, until soft. Stir in the crushed garlic and bay leaf, cooking for another minute.Increase the heat to medium-high, pour in the chicken stock, and bring to a boil. Slice the chicken breasts into thin strips on a cutting board using a sharp knife. Add the chicken strips, reduce the heat to medium, and simmer for about 15 minutes, until the chicken is fully poached and cooked through.

Remove the chicken from the poaching liquid and set aside. Mix the cornstarch with a little water, about 1 teaspoon, to form a paste, then add it to the pan. Bring the soup back to a boil and cook until the soup thickens, about 8 to 10 minutes. Stir in the yogurt and chickpeas, then return the cooked chicken to the pan. Add the crushed red pepper flakes and the lemon juice and season with the salt and pepper. Taste for seasoning, and add more salt and pepper, if desired. Finish by stirring in the cilantro and paprika.

To serve, ladle the soup into individual serving bowls, garnish with the micro greens, if using, and serve warm.

BEVERAGE SUGGESTION

A Ksara Moscatel from the Bekaa Valley in Lebanon pairs elegantly with Lebanese-inspired chickpea and yogurt soup with chicken, chili, and lemon. The wine's floral aromatics and gentle sweetness soften the heat of the chili, while bright acidity mirrors the lemon and enhances the creamy tang of the yogurt.

LIME-KISSED NOPALES

with Onions, Tomatoes, Cilantro & Chipotles

If you've never cooked with cactus before, this salad is the perfect way to start. Nopales—the tender young pads of the prickly pear cactus—bring a bright, tangy flavor and a pleasantly crisp-tender texture that's both surprising and satisfying. Tossed with juicy tomatoes, sharp onions, fresh cilantro, and smoky chipotles, this salad is vibrant and full of character. A generous squeeze of lime adds zing, while creamy avocado offers a cooling contrast.

Serves 6

2 pounds nopales cactus pads, cleaned and chopped
2 tomatoes, diced
1 yellow onion, peeled and chopped
¾ cup chopped fresh cilantro leaves
3 tablespoons puréed canned chipotles in adobo
½ cup fresh lime juice
⅛ teaspoon kosher salt, more to taste
⅛ teaspoon fresh cracked black pepper, more to taste
Sliced avocados, for serving
Warm corn tortillas, for serving

Add about 8 cups salted water to a stockpot over medium-high heat. Bring to a boil, then blanch the nopales in the boiling water for about 10 to 15 minutes. The nopales will become tender and deepen in color when they are done. Cool and drain thoroughly to remove any excess liquid. Note: Nopales have a similar texture to okra and may feel slimy at first, but this will subside after draining.

Cooking with Cactus

The Prickly Star of the Produce Aisle

Nopales—the flat, paddle-shaped leaves of the prickly pear cactus—are a beloved ingredient in Mexican kitchens, prized for their tart flavor and snappy texture. When raw, they have a bit of a slippery quality, but once blanched, their natural viscosity disappears, leaving behind something akin to a cross between green beans and okra, but with a distinctively bold, vegetal edge. Nopales are often available at specialty grocery stores and Mexican markets and can be found in the produce section. Look for firm, bright green pads with minimal blemishes, and slice them into strips or dice before cooking. Their tangy bite makes them the perfect addition to salads, tacos, and even scrambled eggs. Consider this your invitation to embrace the cactus—not just as a garnish, but as the star of the plate.

Add the nopales to a large bowl and add the tomatoes, onions, cilantro, and puréed chipotles, mixing well to incorporate. Season with the lime juice, salt, and pepper. Taste for seasoning, and add more salt and pepper, if desired.

To plate the dish, pile a helping of the salad onto each plate, and top with slices of avocado. Serve with warm tortillas alongside. Serve immediately.

BEVERAGE SUGGESTION

Include a nice glass of Tequila Blanco (my favorite is Casa Noble). Tequila pairs perfectly with lime-kissed nopales, onions, tomatoes, cilantro, and chipotles. The bright citrus and herbal notes in tequila complement the fresh, tangy flavors of the salad, while its smoky, slightly earthy character balances the smoky heat of the chipotles.

Roasted Garlic-Almond Soup

with Pomegranate Seeds

This distinctive soup aligns with many of the elements found in traditional Spanish soups, which often combine simple, high-quality ingredients with bold flavors. Spanish cuisine is known for using aromatic ingredients like garlic, olive oil, and almonds in many of its signature dishes. In fact, ajo blanco, a traditional Andalusian garlic and almond cold soup, shares similar flavors with this dish, where garlic and almonds create a rich, velvety base. The addition of pomegranate seeds in this version introduces a burst of sweetness and acidity, offering a modern twist that contrasts beautifully with the rich, nutty soup.

Serves 4

1 whole head garlic
1 teaspoon, plus 2 tablespoons, olive oil, divided
1 white onion, peeled and chopped
2 ribs celery, chopped
¾ cup blanched almonds
2½ cups chicken stock
1 dried bay leaf
½ cup almond milk
2 tablespoons heavy cream
¼ teaspoon kosher salt, more to taste
¼ teaspoon fresh cracked black pepper, more to taste
Chopped fresh chives, for garnish
Pomegranate seeds, for garnish
Slivered, toasted almonds, for garnish

Preheat the oven to 375°F. Cut the garlic bulb in half, drizzle 1 teaspoon of the olive oil, and wrap it in aluminum foil. Roast for 30 to 40 minutes, or until the garlic is soft and fragrant. Remove from the oven and set aside.

Heat the remaining 2 tablespoons olive oil in a large saucepan over medium heat, until shimmering. Add the chopped onion, celery, and blanched almonds and sauté until soft and lightly browned, about 4 to 5 minutes. Add the chicken stock to the pan and bring to a boil. Unwrap the roasted garlic and squeeze the cloves into the pot. Add the bay leaf and bring the mixture to a simmer, cooking for 10 minutes.

Remove the bay leaf and blend the soup until smooth using an immersion blender, or you can remove it to a high-powered blender or food processor fitted with a blade attachment to blend. Return the soup to the pot, then stir in the almond milk and heavy cream. Season with the salt and pepper, taste for seasoning, and add more, if desired.

To serve, ladle the soup into bowls and garnish each bowl with chopped chives, toasted slivered almonds, and pomegranate seeds. Serve immediately.

BEVERAGE SUGGESTION

I enjoy pairing this dish with a nice Godella like Emilio Moro Polvorete. The wine beautifully complements the roasted garlic-almond soup topped with pomegranate seeds. Its round texture and subtle nuttiness enhance the creamy, savory soup base, as bright acidity and citrus notes lift the dish and contrast with the juicy burst of the pomegranate.

South Indian Lentil & Tomato Rasam

Topped with Crispy Spice-Coated Okra

This vibrant dish is rooted in the culinary traditions of South India. The rasam soup is a tangy and spiced broth made with ripe tomatoes, lentils, curry leaves, and tamarind, creating a rich, savory, and aromatic flavor profile. Fresh curry leaves, rasam powder, and tamarind pulp, incidentally, can all usually be found at specialty Asian grocery stores, or they are available to order online. The dish is further balanced with the warmth of cumin seeds, fresh ginger, and garlic. The addition of tender lentils makes it hearty, while the tamarind pulp lends a zesty tang that cuts through the richness of the soup. To bring our own little dash of Texas flair, the topping of crispy, spice-coated okra adds a crunchy contrast to the smooth and flavorful soup.

Serves 4

Crispy Spice-Coated Okra

Makes about 2 cups

¼ teaspoon ground turmeric
½ teaspoon ground chili powder
¼ teaspoon ground chaat masala
½ cup all-purpose flour
12 medium-size okra, trimmed and thinly sliced
Juice of ½ lemon
Vegetable oil, for frying

South Indian Lentil & Tomato Rasam

2 tablespoons vegetable oil
½ teaspoon whole cumin seeds

1 sprig curry leaves
½ inch fresh ginger piece, peeled and crushed
2 cloves garlic, peeled and crushed
1½ cups well-ripened diced tomatoes
2 tablespoons rasam powder
2 cups water
¾ cup cooked and drained dried lentils
¼ teaspoon kosher salt, more to taste
¼ teaspoon fresh cracked black pepper, more to taste
1 tablespoon tamarind pulp
2 tablespoons chopped fresh cilantro leaves
Pani puri (see sidebar), for garnish, optional

To prepare the Crispy Spice-Coated Okra: Add the tumeric, chili powder, chaat masala, and flour to a small bowl. Mix to combine. Toss the sliced okra in the lemon juice to lightly coat. Then, coat the okra pieces with the flour-spice mixture, tapping off any excess flour. Set aside. Add the vegetable oil to a deep-frying pan so that it is about 1½ inches deep in the pan. Heat over medium-high heat until shimmering, then fry the okra in the oil in batches, until golden brown and crispy, about 3-4 minutes per batch. Drain on paper towels to remove excess oil. Reheat when ready to serve.

To begin the rasam, heat the vegetable oil in a pan over medium heat until shimmering. Add the cumin seeds and cook until they snap, crackle, and turn fragrant, 2 to 3 minutes. Stir in the curry leaves, crushed ginger, and garlic, sautéing briefly until aromatic. Add the diced tomatoes with rasam powder and cook, stirring often, until the tomatoes soften, about 5 minutes. Pour in the water and stir in the cooked lentils. Season with salt and pepper, adjusting to taste. Bring the soup to a simmer and cook gently for about 30 minutes, letting the flavors meld together. Finally, stir in the tamarind pulp for brightness and remove from the heat. To plate the dish, ladle the hot rasam into bowls, then top with a handful of Crispy Spice-Coated Okra and a sprinkle of fresh cilantro. Garnish with some pani puri, if using, and serve.

From South India with Love

The Ritual of Rasam

Rasam is far more than just soup—it's a cornerstone of South Indian cooking and comfort, often enjoyed daily in Tamil, Telugu, Kannada, and Malayali households. The name rasam comes from the Sanskrit word rasa, meaning "essence" or "juice," which speaks to the dish's deep, spiced broth and its soul-soothing qualities. Traditionally made with tamarind, tomatoes, and spices like cumin, black pepper, and mustard seeds, rasam is beloved for its bold tanginess and medicinal warmth—long praised as a go-to remedy for colds or upset stomachs. What also sets rasam apart is its adaptability: it can be sipped on its own, ladled over rice, or served as part of a multi-course South Indian meal. While countless regional variations exist, the core idea is always the same—transforming humble ingredients into a deeply flavorful, aromatic broth that wakes up the palate and comforts the spirit.

BEVERAGE SUGGESTION

A lightly oaked Chardonnay like Macon Villages works wonders with South Indian lentil and tomato rasam topped with crispy spice-coated okra. The wine's creamy texture and subtle vanilla notes balance the bright acidity and spice of the rasam, while its medium body complements the crunchy, flavorful okra without overpowering the dish.

What is Pani Puri?

Pani puri (also known as *pain puri*, *pani poori*, or *golgappa*) is a popular Indian street snack made of hollow, crispy puri shells filled with a mixture of flavored water (called *pani*), tamarind chutney, spiced mashed potatoes or chickpeas, and sometimes onions or sprouts.

The puris are small, round, and light, and when you pop one into your mouth, the tangy, spicy, and refreshing flavored water bursts out, creating a delicious explosion of flavors and textures—crunchy, tangy, spicy, and slightly sweet all at once. It's a fun, interactive snack loved across India and beyond!

Stuffed Lebanese Zucchini

with Tender Lamb, Pine Nuts & Paprika Yogurt Cheese

This is a classic and comforting Lebanese dish: small, tender zucchini are hollowed out and stuffed with a flavorful mixture of ground lamb, onions, tomatoes, and earthy za'atar—a Middle Eastern spice blend made with thyme, sesame seeds, and sumac. The seasoned stuffing also includes pine nuts for added texture and flavor. To finish, it's served with a homemade soft yogurt cheese called shanklish over top. The combination of the warm, savory lamb filling, the slightly sweet zucchini, and the tangy yogurt creates a well-balanced and harmonious meal.

Serves 4

Shanklish Paprika Yogurt Cheese

Makes about 2 dozen small balls

12 cups plain yogurt

1 cup water

2 teaspoons smoked ground paprika

1 teaspoon crushed red pepper flakes

1 teaspoon kosher salt

Stuffed Lebanese Zucchini

4 medium zucchinis

1 tablespoon olive oil, plus extra for brushing

½ teaspoon kosher salt, divided

½ teaspoon fresh cracked black pepper, divided

2 pounds 80/20 ground lamb

1 white onion, peeled and finely chopped

2 cloves garlic, peeled and finely minced

1 tablespoon za'atar
3 to 4 tomatoes, peeled and chopped
½ cup toasted pine nuts
Micro red shiso leaves, for garnish, optional

To make the Shanklish Paprika Yogurt Cheese: Add the yogurt, water, smoked ground paprika, crushed red pepper flakes, and the kosher salt to a large heavy pot over medium heat. Slowly bring to a boil, stirring only occasionally to avoid sticking, but allowing the cheese curds to form. Once the curds begin to form and separate from the milky whey, about 45 minutes, remove from the heat. Layer a colander over a large bowl and line the colander with cheesecloth. Strain the curd from the whey by pouring it through the cheesecloth. Allow the cheese to cool and drain in the colander for 10 to 15 minutes. Once the cheese is cool enough to handle, shape the cheese into small balls with your hands. Note: If you prefer a smoother texture, you can pulse the mixture in a food processor before shaping. Transfer the cheese to an airtight container and refrigerate for at least 2 hours before serving. Any leftovers can be stored in the refrigerator for up to 1 week.

Preheat the oven to 375°F.

Wash the zucchini and cut each in half. Brush the zucchini with olive oil and then season with ¼ teaspoon each salt and pepper. Place in the oven on a roasting pan and roast for 15 minutes until soft. Remove from the oven, allow to cool for a few minutes, and then hollow out the seeds, creating an oblong-shaped pocket for the stuffing. Place the zucchini back in the roasting pan and reserve.

While the zucchini is roasting, brown the lamb in a large sauté pan over medium-high heat, breaking the lamb into small pieces with the back of a cooking utensil. Sauté until the lamb is cooked through, about 5 to 8 minutes, then add the onion and garlic. Sauté for an additional 2 to 3 minutes, until the onions are soft and translucent, and the garlic is fragrant. Add the za'atar and the tomatoes, stir to combine, and then let the lamb mixture cook at a low simmer for about 30 minutes, until thick and saucy.

Layers of Flavor, Roots of Home

Lebanon's Love for Mehshi

In Lebanese kitchens like my grandmother's, stuffed vegetables—known as mehshi—are a deeply rooted tradition, often made in large batches and shared with family over long, leisurely meals. Zucchini, or kousa, is a beloved choice for stuffing due to its delicate flavor and tender texture. The filling typically combines seasoned ground meat like the lamb found here, plus rice or bulgur, and warm spices like cinnamon or za'atar. What sets this dish apart is its balance: the richness of lamb, the crunch of pine nuts, and the brightness of herbs and tomatoes come together in perfect harmony. Topped with tangy yogurt cheese like shanklish, it's a dish that celebrates the Levantine love of bold flavors and warm hospitality—all wrapped in a humble zucchini.

Check for seasoning and add the additional ¼ teaspoon each of salt and pepper, as desired. Remove from the heat and allow to cool for 5 minutes.

Divide the lamb mixture among the zucchini halves, filling each of the zucchini with a generous helping. Top each with several curds of the Shanklish Paprika Yogurt Cheese and then roast in the oven for 30 minutes, until the cheese is bubbly and melted over top. Remove from the oven and top with zucchini, a sprinkle of pine nuts and the micro greens, if using, and serve.

BEVERAGE SUGGESTION

A medium-bodied French Grenache or Côtes du Rhône red pairs beautifully with stuffed Lebanese zucchini filled with tender lamb, pine nuts, and paprika yogurt cheese. The wine's ripe red fruit and subtle spice complement the lamb's richness and paprika's smoky warmth, while its moderate tannins balance the creamy yogurt cheese and the earthiness of the zucchini.

ROOTS & TUBERS

I've always had a soft spot for roots and tubers—they're the kind of ingredients that feel like home. Humble, hearty, and full of potential, they bring a natural richness and comfort to the plate. In these recipes, I've taken some of my favorite foundational ingredients and given them bold new life. From velvety butternut squash bisque to tender, spiced potato dumplings, these dishes are rooted in tradition but reimagined with a fresh, flavorful twist. Earthy, creamy, crispy, and fragrant, each bite is a reminder of how these grounded vegetables can elevate any table. Whether folded into pillowy gnocchi or crisped up as golden fritters, these vegetables also show their versatility across cuisines and cultures. I love how they can be silky, crunchy, aromatic, or fiery—sometimes all in the same dish. These are the kind of recipes that invite you to slow down, savor deeply, and enjoy the simple luxury of comfort food with global flair.

Creamy Butternut Squash Bisque

with Chorizo-Corn Fritters & Chili Crème Fraîche

This beautiful layered, texture-rich dish turns a simple preparation into something memorable. The base is classic comfort: slow-simmered squash puréed into a silky, golden soup laced with cream and Parmesan. But things get interesting with the toppings. Crispy cornmeal fritters studded with smoky Spanish chorizo and sweet corn bring crunch, heat, and serious depth, while a dollop of chipotle-laced crème fraîche cuts through the richness with a tangy, spicy finish. Every bite balances creamy, crispy, sweet, and spicy—like the best parts of fall packed into one bold, belly-warming bowl.

Serves 6

Chili Crème Fraîche

Makes 1 cup

1 cup crème fraîche or sour cream
1 chipotle pepper in adobo, finely chopped
1 teaspoon lime juice, more to taste
1/8 teaspoon kosher salt, more to taste

Roasted Butternut Squash Bisque

3 tablespoons extra-virgin olive oil
1 yellow or white onion, peeled and thinly sliced
4 cloves garlic, peeled and smashed
2 teaspoons kosher salt, divided
1/4 teaspoon fresh cracked black pepper
1 medium (about 2 pounds) butternut squash, peeled, seeded, and cubed
4 cups chicken broth or water
2 tablespoons freshly grated Parmigiano-Reggiano cheese

1 cup heavy cream
Micro cilantro, for garnish, optional

Chorizo-Corn Fritters

Makes about 10 to 12 fritters

1¼ cups all-purpose flour
1¼ cups cornmeal
2 teaspoons baking powder
1 teaspoon kosher salt
1 cup milk
2 large eggs, gently beaten
¼ cup melted unsalted butter
½ cup fresh or frozen corn kernels
½ cup chopped Spanish chorizo
Neutral flavored oil, such as vegetable or canola oil, for frying

To make the Chili Crème Fraîche: Add the crème fraîche and chopped chipotle pepper to a small bowl and whisk well to combine. Stir in the lime juice and salt. Taste for seasoning, and add more lime juice and salt, if desired. Cover and chill until ready to use. Note: This gets even better after 30 minutes in the fridge, so plan to prepare this one ahead. Leftovers can also be stored in an airtight container in the refrigerator for 2 to 3 days.

To make the Bisque: Add the olive oil to a soup pot over medium heat. Once the oil is shimmering, add the sliced onion, smashed garlic, 1 teaspoon of the salt, and the black pepper. Cook, covered, stirring occasionally, until the onions are soft and fragrant, about 5 minutes. Add the butternut squash and the remaining teaspoon of salt, continuing to cook for about 12 minutes, until the squash is tender. Pour in the chicken broth, bring the mixture to a simmer, and cook uncovered for about 20 minutes, until all the vegetables are tender. Set aside to cool slightly.

Purée the soup until smooth using an immersion blender, or you can transfer it to a high-powered blender or a food processor fitted with a blade attachment, and purée in batches. Return the soup to the pot, if necessary, stir in the grated cheese and heavy cream, and reheat gently over medium heat until silky-smooth. Keep warm until ready to serve.

To make the Chorizo-Corn Fritters: Add the flour, cornmeal, baking powder, salt, milk, beaten eggs, melted butter, corn kernels, and chopped chirizo to a medium bowl. Mix until well combined. Add oil to a frying pan or Dutch oven to a level of about 1½ inches deep in the pot. Heat over medium-high heat until the oil is shimmering. Use a tablespoon or ice cream scoop to ladle out small spoonfuls of the fritter mixture and carefully drop them into the oil. Fry, in batches, for about 2 to 4 minutes each, or until golden brown. Turn the fritters once for even cooking. Remove from the oil and drain on paper towels. Serve immediately.

To serve, ladle the warm bisque into bowls, top with one to two Chorizo-Corn Fritters, garnish with the micro cilantro, if using, and finish with a dollop of the Chili Crème Fraîche.

BEVERAGE SUGGESTION

A rich, creamy butternut squash bisque with chorizo-corn fritters and chili crème fraîche works well with a lightly oaked Sonoma Chardonnay or a spicy German Gewürztraminer. The Chardonnay's buttery texture and balanced acidity complement the bisque's creaminess, while Gewürztraminer's aromatic spice and slight sweetness balance the smoky heat of the chorizo and chili crème fraîche.

Handmade Spinach-Potato Gnocchi

in Gorgonzola Cream

This dish is a cozy indulgence with a touch of elegance—handmade spinach gnocchi bathed in a silky gorgonzola cream that clings to every ridge and curve. The spinach brings a hint of earthiness and color, while the potatoes keep things light and pillowy. A whisper of nutmeg and Parmesan round out the flavor, making each bite both familiar and unexpected. This is a recipe that speaks to the joy of making things from scratch—rolling, shaping, tasting, and savoring. Serve it on its own or add your favorite protein for a meal that's comforting, soulful, and beautifully delicate.

Serves 4

Gorgonzola Cream

Makes about 2 cups

2 cups heavy cream

¼ cup gorgonzola cheese

Spinach-Potato Gnocchi

4 tablespoons kosher salt, divided

1 pound russet potatoes, washed and scrubbed

4 cups fresh spinach leaves

3 to 4 large egg yolks

½ cup freshly grated Parmigiano-Reggiano cheese

¼ teaspoon freshly grated or ground nutmeg

½ teaspoon gray sea salt

¼ teaspoon fresh cracked black pepper

1 cup all-purpose flour, divided, plus more for dusting board and dough

To make the Gorgonzola Cream: Add the cream to a small saucepan over medium heat. Bring the cream to just about simmering, then stir in the gorgonzola cheese. Bring to a simmer and allow the cheese to melt into the cream, about 1 minute. Continue to simmer until the mixture thickens and reduces slightly, another 3 to 4 minutes. Then turn off the heat and allow to cool slightly before use. Chef's tip: This sauce is best served fresh to ensure it maintains its beautifully smooth texture. I would recommend preparing it at the same time you cook your finished gnocchi on the stovetop.

Preheat the oven to 425°F.

Spread 2 tablespoons of the kosher salt in a thin layer on a baking sheet and arrange the potatoes on top. Bake the potatoes until a bit overcooked, about 45 minutes. Let sit until cool enough to handle, cut in half, and scoop out the flesh. Reserve the potato skins, if desired, for another use.

While the potatoes are cooking, prep the spinach purée: Wash and dry the spinach and then add to a saucepan over medium heat. Add 1 teaspoon water, then cook the spinach for 2 to 3 minutes, or until the spinach has wilted. Cool slightly, then blend with a food processor or hand blender. If necessary, you can add a little water or milk to reach a smooth purée. You should have about ½ cup spinach purée once finished.

Prep the gnocchi: Pass the potatoes through a potato ricer or grate them on the large holes of a box grater. You should have about 2 cups. Make a mound of potatoes on the counter with a well in the middle; add 3 of the egg yolks, the cheese, nutmeg, gray sea salt, and pepper. Add in the reserved spinach purée. Fold in the well ingredients with the potatoes, mixing well with your hands. Sprinkle ½ cup of the flour over the potatoes and, using your knuckles, press it into the potatoes. Fold the mass over on itself and press down again. Sprinkle on more flour, little by little, folding and pressing the dough until it just holds together. Note: Try not to knead it; use a light touch. Work any dough clinging to your fingers back into the dough. If the mixture is too dry, add the last egg yolk or a little water. The dough should give under slight pressure. It will feel firm but yielding. To test if the dough is the correct consistency, take a piece and roll it with your hands on a well-floured board into a rope ½-inch in diameter. If the dough holds together, it is ready. If not, add more flour, fold and press the dough several more times, and test again.

Lightly flour your work surface and dough, then cut the dough into 4 pieces. Roll each into ropes about ½ inch thick and cut into ½-inch lengths. Dust the gnocchi with flour as you cut. You can cook the gnocchi as is or shape them using a gnocchi board, butter paddle, or fork. To shape, set the board at a 45-degree angle, press each piece gently with your thumb, and roll it away so it curls, forming ridges on the outside and a smooth inner curve. The indentation helps the gnocchi cook quickly and catch sauce. Place the shaped gnocchi on floured, parchment-lined baking sheets. When ready to cook, bring a large pot of water to a boil, add 2 tablespoons kosher salt, and drop in the gnocchi. Cook about 90 seconds from the time they float to the surface. Lift out with a skimmer, shaking off excess water.

To serve, transfer the gnocchi to a large serving bowl and spoon over the Gorgonzola Cream. Serve warm, with extra cracked black pepper and grated Parmigiano-Reggiano cheese, as desired.

BEVERAGE SUGGESTION

Handmade spinach-potato gnocchi in Gorgonzola cream pairs well with Viognier; its richness and creamy texture balance tangy cheese, while fruit and oak complement earthy spinach-potato flavors.

Spiced Beef-Filled Potato Dumplings

with Creamy Coconut Curry Soup

This dish is my take on comfort food—with a bold, cross-cultural twist. Fluffy Yukon Gold potato dumplings, stuffed with smoky spiced ground beef, are either baked until golden or crisp-fried for a little extra indulgence. They're served floating in a rich coconut curry broth that's fragrant, warming, and just a touch tropical. It's part Southern grit, part global flavor, and all heart—exactly the kind of dish that defines the kitchen at Salum.

Serves 8

Creamy Coconut Curry Soup

Makes 6 cups

1 yellow onion, peeled and diced
3 cloves garlic, peeled and finely diced
3 tablespoons yellow curry powder
2 (13½-ounce) cans unsweetened coconut milk
4 cups chicken stock
¼ teaspoon kosher salt, more to taste
¼ teaspoon fresh cracked black pepper, more to taste

Spiced Beef-Filled Potato Dumplings

6 unpeeled Yukon Gold potatoes
3 cloves garlic, peeled
1 cup heavy cream
½ cup unsalted butter

½ teaspoon kosher salt, divided
½ teaspoon fresh cracked black pepper, divided
½ pound 80/20 ground beef
1 cup peeled and diced white onion
¼ teaspoon cayenne pepper, more for garnish
¼ teaspoon ground cumin
Cooking spray, if baking
All-purpose flour, if frying
Neutral flavored oil, such as vegetable or canola, if frying
Edible micro flowers, for garnish, optional

To make the Creamy Coconut Soup: Add the diced onion and garlic to a large pot set over medium heat and sauté until translucent and fragrant, about 2 to 3 minutes. Stir in the curry powder and cook for 2 to 3 more minutes, allowing the spices to bloom. Add the coconut milk and chicken stock, then season with the salt and pepper. Let the soup simmer until it thickens and is creamy in texture. Taste for seasoning, and add more salt and pepper, if desired. The soup can be prepared up to 2 days ahead of time and stored in an airtight container in the refrigerator; gently rewarm before using.

Add the potatoes and garlic to a large pot and fill the pot with enough water to cover. Set over medium-high heat and bring to a low boil, cooking until the potatoes and garlic are tender, about 15 minutes. Drain the water and return the pot to the heat. Add the heavy cream, butter, and season with ¼ teaspoon each salt and pepper, stirring until the butter is melted. Remove from the heat and allow the mixture to cool for a few minutes, then mash with a wire masher until smooth and firm. Note: If the mixture is runny at all, add a bit of cornstarch or flour to thicken.

Add the ground beef to a separate pan over medium heat and sauté the ground beef with the diced onion, cayenne pepper, and cumin, until the beef is cooked through, about 5 to 6 minutes. Season with the remaining salt and pepper, adding more to taste, if desired. Drain any excess fat from the pan.

To form the dumplings, place a spoonful of potato purée in the palm of your hand. Add a small amount of the cooked beef mixture in the center and cover with more potato purée, shaping it into a small oval. Set the dumplings aside on baking sheet.

The dumplings can either be baked in the oven or breaded and deep-fried for a crispy exterior. To bake: Preheat the oven to 350°F. Arrange the dumplings on a baking sheet, and spray lightly with cooking spray. Bake the dumplings for about 20 minutes, or until golden brown. Remove from the oven and allow to cool for several minutes before serving.

To fry: Add oil to a large frying pan so that it is about 1½ inches deep in the pan. Bring the oil up to temperature over medium-high heat, until shimmering. Lightly coat dumplings in flour, tapping off any excess to ensure you have a nice, even layer. Carefully add a few dumplings at a time to the oil, allowing them plenty of space to cook, and fry in batches until golden brown, about 2 to 3 minutes each. Remove the dumplings with a slotted spoon and place on a paper towel-lined plate for several minutes to allow excess oil to drain before serving.

To serve, place one to two dumplings in each bowl and ladle the soup around it. Garnish with a sprinkle of cayenne pepper and edible micro flowers, if using, and serve immediately.

Starch & Spice

Why Potatoes + Curry Are Oh-So Nice

There's a reason you'll find potatoes swimming happily in curries from Mumbai to Mexico City: the humble tuber is a master at soaking up flavor. Mild, starchy, and grounding, potatoes act as a blank canvas that gives bold, spiced sauces like curry room to shine without ever competing. In Indian, Thai, Caribbean, and even British curries, potatoes add heartiness and texture while taming heat and stretching sauces. Their creaminess balances sharper, acidic notes like ginger, tamarind, or tomato, and they hold up beautifully to long simmering or even a quick fry. Whether mashed into dumplings, tucked into stews, or roasted to soak up golden spice, potatoes make the perfect partner in this warm, aromatic union.

Beverage Suggestion

For this soup, a Belgian style saison or a Hefeweizen is an excellent pairing. The saison's fruity, peppery notes and lively carbonation cut through the richness and complement the spice, while a Hefeweizen's creamy wheat character and subtle clove and banana flavors balance the coconut's creaminess and the curry's warmth.

Yellow Beet-Oat Fritters

with Fresh Lemon, Mint & Dill

In every recipe I create, I make sure to incorporate vegetables—not just for their flavor and texture but also for their incredible health benefits. These yellow beet-oat fritters are a perfect example. Packed with nutrients and bursting with flavor, they offer a delightful balance of crunch on the outside and softness on the inside, making them a wholesome and satisfying bite.

Serves 4

¾ cup old-fashioned rolled oats
2 medium yellow beets, peeled and grated
1 teaspoon kosher salt
2 large eggs
1 cup crumbled queso fresco
2 tablespoons chopped fresh dill fronds, plus extra for serving
2 tablespoons chopped fresh mint leaves, plus extra for serving
1 teaspoon cayenne pepper
½ cup extra-virgin olive oil
Juice from 1 large lemon, for garnish

Finely chop the oats in a food processor and remove to a large bowl. Meanwhile, toss the grated yellow beets with the teaspoon of salt in another bowl and then place the yellow beets in a colander. Set in the sink to drain. After 5 minutes, carefully press down on the beets to remove any excess liquid. Add the yellow beets with the oats in the bowl, and add the eggs, queso fresco, dill, mint, and the cayenne pepper, mixing well to combine.

Yellow Beets

Sunshine from the Soil

Often overshadowed by their deep red cousins, yellow (or golden) beets deserve a spotlight of their own—especially in these crispy, herb-flecked fritters. Milder and slightly sweeter in flavor, they won't stain your cutting board—or your fingertips—and they pair beautifully with bright herbs, citrus, and tangy cheeses, as showcased here with lemon, dill, mint, and queso fresco. Nutritionally, yellow beets are rich in fiber, potassium, and immune-boosting vitamin C, and they're packed with antioxidants that support heart health and reduce inflammation. Their sunny hue comes from betalains, plant compounds known for their detoxifying properties. Folded into these fritters, they bring not only a golden glow and gentle earthiness, but a satisfying, nutrient-dense crunch in every bite.

Heat the oil in a frying pan over medium-high heat until shimmering. Scoop about ¼ cup of yellow beet batter for each fritter. Note: An ice cream scoop works well for this. Drop the fritters into the oil one or two at a time and cook for about 2 minutes on each side, flipping and cooking until both sides are crisp and golden brown. Remove the fritters with a slotted spoon and drain on a paper towel–lined plate.

To serve, garnish the fritters with a few teaspoons of fresh dill and mint, and a squeeze of lemon juice. Serve warm.

BEVERAGE SUGGESTION

This dish is a perfect match with a crisp, herbal New Zealand Sauvignon Blanc or a light, zesty dry French rosé. These wines' bright acidity and fresh citrus and herbaceous notes enhance the earthiness of the beets while complementing the brightness of the lemon and herbs.

Yukon Gold Potato & Onion Tortilla Española

with Classic Aioli

Tortilla Española is a classic Spanish dish, beloved for its simple yet delicious combination of eggs, potatoes, and onions. In Spain, nearly every home has a tortilla ready to slice, whether for tapas, a quick snack, or a satisfying meal. My grandmother made the best Tortilla Española—perfectly golden, tender, and full of flavor. Comforting and savory, this staple brings people together, no matter the occasion.

Serves 6

Classic Aioli

Makes about 1 cup

1 whole large egg
4 cloves garlic, peeled and minced
2 teaspoons lemon juice
½ cup canola or vegetable oil
½ cup extra-virgin olive oil
⅛ teaspoon kosher salt, more to taste
⅛ teaspoon fresh cracked black pepper, more to taste

Yukon Gold Potato & Onion Tortilla Española

8 large eggs
½ teaspoon kosher salt, divided
2 cups extra-virgin olive oil
1½ pounds Yukon Gold potatoes, peeled, halved, and thinly sliced
2 yellow onions, peeled and thinly sliced

To make the Classic Aioli: Add the egg, garlic, and lemon juice to a blender or food processor. Start the blender and slowly add in the oil, starting with the vegetable or canola oil, and then moving on to the olive oil. Blend until the oil is emulsified. Season with salt and pepper, adding more to taste, as desired. Store in the refrigerator until ready to use. Any leftovers can be stored in an airtight container in the refrigerator for up to 2 weeks.

To begin preparing the tortilla, add the eggs to a large bowl and beat vigorously with ¼ teaspoon of salt until frothy. Set aside.

Add the oil to a large nonstick, oven-safe skillet over medium-high heat. Once the oil is shimmering, add the potatoes and onions, and cook for 20 minutes, or until tender, stirring occasionally. Drain the excess oil into a heatproof bowl, transfer potatoes and onions into a mixing bowl, and season generously with the remaining ¼ teaspoon of salt.

Once the potato and onions are cool to the touch, add them to the beaten eggs in the bowl. Add 3 tablespoons of the reserved frying oil back into the skillet. Heat over medium-high heat until shimmering. Scrape egg mixture into skillet and cook, swirling and shaking pan rapidly, until bottom and sides begin to set, about 3 minutes. Using a heatproof spatula, press the edges in to begin to form the tortilla's signature puck shape. Continue to cook, adjusting the heat as needed to prevent the bottom of the tortilla from burning, until it is beginning to set around the edges, about 3 minutes longer.

Working over a sink or garbage can, place a large overturned flat plate on top of the skillet, and set a hand on top. Note: During this next step, use a dish towel or oven mitt if you are sensitive to heat. Then, in one very quick motion, invert the tortilla onto the plate. Add 1 more tablespoon of the reserved oil to the skillet and return to the heat. Carefully slide the tortilla back into the skillet and continue to cook until the second side is beginning to firm up, about 2 minutes. Use the rubber spatula to again press the sides in all around to form a rounded puck shape. Continue to cook the tortilla until lightly browned on the second side but still tender in the center when pressed with a finger, about 2 minutes longer. Carefully slide the tortilla out of the skillet and onto a clean plate and let stand for at least 5 minutes.

Slice into wedges and serve warm with Classic Aioli.

BEVERAGE SUGGESTION

Try a dry or slightly herbal Yzaguirre vermouth with the tortilla Española. The vermouth's complex botanicals and subtle bitterness brighten the richness of the tortilla and cut through the creamy aioli, while the aromatic herbs echo the dish's savory simplicity for a balanced, flavorful match.

BREADS, GRAINS & RICE

For me, this chapter is a celebration of foundational comforts—the breads we break, the grains we gather around, the rice dishes that bring people together from coast to coast and continent to continent. I've always been drawn to the quiet magic of these ingredients: the way a pot of rice can center a meal, or how the scent of something baking can fill a kitchen with anticipation and warmth. From flaky Southern-style buttermilk biscuits to golden Pan de Muerto glazed with orange, from saffron-scented paella to Veracruz-style rice, these recipes are rooted in tradition but come to life with bold, layered flavors. Whether sweet or savory, baked or simmered, humble or celebratory, these are the dishes I turn to when I want to feel grounded. I love how grains and starches carry the stories of so many cultures. Toasty panzanella with heirloom tomatoes, cheddar-and-Andouille biscuits with whipped maple butter—each bite is full of flavor, memory, and the kind of nourishment that feeds more than just hunger. It feeds connection.

Andouille Sausage, Cheddar & Mustard Biscuits

with Whipped Maple Butter

Whether you're serving them at brunch, alongside a bowl of chili, or just on their own, these biscuits bring serious comfort with a little Southern swagger. Smoky Andouille sausage, sharp cheddar cheese, and tangy whole grain mustard get folded into my signature biscuit dough, creating a savory bite with just the right amount of kick. Served warm with a generous swipe of whipped maple butter, they hit every note: spicy, salty, cheesy, and sweet.

Makes 24 biscuits

Whipped Maple Butter

Makes 3 cups

2 cups softened unsalted butter

1½ cups pure maple syrup

Andouille Sausage, Cheddar & Mustard Biscuits

3 cups all-purpose flour

1 cup grated extra sharp cheddar cheese

¼ cup chopped chives

1 tablespoon baking powder

¾ teaspoon baking soda

¾ teaspoon garlic powder

¾ teaspoon kosher salt

1 teaspoon fresh cracked black pepper

¾ cup cold unsalted butter

1¾ cup cultured buttermilk
3 tablespoons whole grain mustard
1 cup finely chopped and cooked spicy Andouille sausage
Honey, for serving, optional

To make the Whipped Maple Butter: Add the butter to the bowl of an electric mixer fitted with a whisk attachment. Turn the mixer on to medium speed and begin to whip the butter. Then, with the mixer running, drizzle in the maple syrup, occasionally scraping down any butter from the sides of the bowl with a spatula. Mix until the butter is well-combined, light, and airy. Reserve until ready to use. The butter can be prepared up to 1 week in advance, stored in an airtight container in the refrigerator. Bring back to room temperature before use.

Preheat the oven to 400°F.

Add the flour, cheese, chives, baking powder, baking soda, garlic powder, salt, and pepper to a large mixing bowl and stir together. Slice the butter into tablespoon-sized pieces and add the butter to the dry ingredients in the mixing bowl. Mix well. Pour in the buttermilk and stir until the ingredients are incorporated and a rough dough forms. Gently fold in the chopped sausage.

Line a few baking sheets with parchment paper or Silpat. Using a tablespoon or ice cream scoop, drop the batter by the spoonful onto the baking sheets, spacing them out so that they have room to expand during cooking. Bake the biscuits in the oven for 14 to 18 minutes, until cooked through in the middle and golden brown. Remove from the oven. Serve warm with Whipped Maple Butter and honey, if using, on the side.

To make the Orange Glaze: Add the sugar, orange juice, and orange zest to a small saucepan over medium-high heat. Bring the mixture to a boil, stirring occasionally, until the sugar is dissolved into the liquid and the mixture thickens slightly, about 4 to 5 minutes. Remove from the heat and set aside to cool. The glaze can be prepared up to 3 to 4 days ahead of time, stored in an airtight container in the fridge. Bring back to room temperature before use.

Add 1½ cups of the flour to a large mixing bowl, setting the rest aside for later. Add the sugar, yeast and salt, and stir gently to combine. Set aside.

Add the milk, butter, and water to a medium saucepan over medium heat, stirring to combine. Once the butter is melted, remove from the heat and pour the contents of the saucepan into the mixing bowl with the dry ingredients. Stir well to combine. Add in the eggs one at a time, mixing well in between each one to incorporate.

Continue mixing while you slowly add the other 3½ cups flour. Note: You can use an electric mixer, if desired, as it can be quite hard work to do by hand once the dough thickens. Either way, if the mixture seems too wet after adding the allotted amount of flour, keep adding in bits of flour, until the dough is soft and just slightly sticky in consistency.

Transfer the dough to a floured board and knead for 10 minutes until it is smooth, elastic, and stretchy. Put the dough in a greased bowl, cover with plastic wrap, and allow to rise and double in size. This should take about 90 minutes. Note: If you put the bowl in a warm location, such as a sunny windowsill, it will help the dough rise.

Preheat the oven to 350°F. Once the dough has doubled in size, remove it from the bowl and place back on a lightly floured surface. Cut the dough in half. Then cut away about a cup of the dough with a knife and set aside. Lightly flour your hands, then shape the two dough balls into loaves. Then, pinch off pieces of the reserved dough and roll them into strips. Layer the strips of dough on top of each loaf in a crisscross pattern, so that they resemble bones.

Pan de Muerto

Bread for the Spirits

Pan de Muerto, or "Bread of the Dead," is a sweet, fragrant bread traditionally baked for Día de los Muertos, the Mexican holiday celebrating and honoring deceased loved ones. Its round shape symbolizes the cycle of life and death, while the decorative bone-shaped dough pieces on top represent the souls of the departed. This bread is often flavored with orange blossom water, anise, or cinnamon, giving it a subtle, aromatic sweetness that perfectly balances its soft, slightly dense texture. As the holiday is a joyful celebration of memory and life, Pan de Muerto plays a key role in the altar offerings, or ofrendas, alongside marigolds, candles, and photographs of the deceased. Beyond its spiritual significance, the bread also serves as a delightful treat enjoyed by families during the festivities. Each region of Mexico has its own variation on the recipe, with slight differences in shape, texture, and decoration, but the central idea remains the same: a sweet, sacred bread that connects the living to the departed.

Put the bread loaves on two separate lightly greased baking sheets and bake in the oven for 20 to 40 minutes, depending on the size of your loaves and the type of oven you have. Rotate the loaves between top and bottom racks about halfway through and be sure to check the bread at regular intervals. Once they are a nice, golden-brown color on top, and sound hollow when you tap them, they are done.

Remove from the oven and allow to cool for a few minutes. Brush both loaves with the Orange Glaze. Slice and serve warm.

BEVERAGE SUGGESTION

Pan de muerto paired with hot chocolate is a classic Mexican combination that's pure comfort. The slightly sweet, aromatic bread complements the rich, creamy, and spiced warmth of traditional Mexican hot chocolate, creating a cozy balance of flavors that's perfect for celebrating Día de los Muertos or any cozy moment.

Panzanella Salad with Heirloom Tomatoes

and Black Truffle Parmesan Crisps

Born out of cucina povera—the Italian tradition of making the most of humble ingredients—panzanella is a Tuscan bread salad that transforms stale bread and ripe tomatoes into something deeply flavorful and satisfying. This version stays true to its roots, using rustic, day-old bread to soak up the juices of peak-season heirloom tomatoes, a sharp vinegar dressing, and sweet red onions. The crisp is what makes this one distinctive: a lacy round of Parmigiano-Reggiano infused with black truffle, baked until golden, and just brittle enough to shatter over the top. For the canned truffle peels, they can often be found at specialty grocers or are readily available to order online.

Serves 4

Black Truffle Parmesan Crisps

Makes 4 large crisps

2 cups grated Parmigiano-Reggiano cheese
2 teaspoons truffle peels
1 teaspoon truffle oil

Panzanella Salad with Heirloom Tomatoes

2 large heirloom tomatoes
4 cups stale country-style Italian bread
3/4 cup peeled and thinly sliced red onions
1 clove garlic, peeled and minced
2 tablespoons red wine vinegar
1/4 cup extra-virgin Italian olive oil

½ cup fresh basil leaves
¼ teaspoon kosher salt, more to taste
¼ teaspoon fresh cracked black pepper, more to taste

To make the Black Truffle Parmesan Crisps: Preheat the oven to a 350°F. Add the grated cheese, truffle peels, and truffle oil to a small bowl and mix together. On a sheet pan lined with parchment paper, divide the cheese mixture into 4 equal portions and form them into circles. Bake in the oven until the cheese melts and lightly browns, about 5 to 7 minutes. Let the crisps cool to room temperature before serving.

Slice heirloom tomatoes into bite-sized wedges and place in a large mixing bowl. Remove any crusts from the stale bread and cut into bite-sized cubes. Add the bread to the tomatoes in the bowl, then toss in the sliced red onion. Set aside.

Whisk together the garlic, red wine vinegar, and olive oil in a separate small bowl, then pour the dressing over the bread mixture. Let sit at room temperature for 30 minutes to allow the flavors to meld.

Wash and dry the basil, then tear the leaves into pieces. Toss the basil into the panzanella, and season with the salt and pepper. Taste for seasoning and add more, if desired. To serve, heap a helping of the panzanella onto each plate, then top each with a Black Truffle Parmesan crisp. Serve immediately.

Salum-Style Saffron Paella

with Mussels, Pork Shoulder & Piquillo Peppers

This classic dish bursts with a variety of textures and flavors on the palate—tender meat, briny seafood, fresh veggies, and a crispy, caramelized layer of rice at the bottom called the socarrat, which is highly prized by paella lovers. There are many variations of traditional paella, but it is most famous in two styles: paella Valenciana, which typically includes rabbit, chicken, and vegetables, and paella de mariscos, which showcases the bounty of the sea. My version combines the best of both versions, plus boasts a little extra Texas flair thanks to the addition of hearty pork shoulder and smoky piquillo peppers.

Serves 6

4 tablespoons extra-virgin olive oil
½ pound boneless pork shoulder
¼ cup diced yellow onion
2 tablespoons chopped garlic
1 cup sliced piquillo peppers
1 cup Bomba, Calasparra, or Arborio rice
2 cups chicken stock or broth
½ tablespoon saffron threads
12 large peeled and deveined shrimp
12 cleaned mussels
½ pound Spanish chorizo, sliced into rounds
½ teaspoon kosher salt
½ teaspoon fresh cracked black pepper
1 cup fresh peas

SAFFRON

Liquid Gold of the Mediterranean

Saffron is one of the world's most prized spices, both for its unique flavor and vibrant golden hue. Originating in the Mediterranean region, saffron comes from the delicate red stigmas of the crocus sativus flower. Each flower only produces three tiny threads, and it takes thousands of flowers to yield just one pound of saffron, making it one of the most labor-intensive and expensive spices to harvest. The process is painstaking: the threads are carefully handpicked during the short flowering season, typically in autumn, and must be dried immediately to preserve their flavor and color. To unlock saffron's full potential in your cooking, it's essential to bloom the threads before using them. This is done by soaking the saffron in warm water or broth, either before use in your recipe, or worked into the process as seen here in this paella. This process allows the saffron to release its aromatic oils and vibrant color, infusing your dish with both a deep, floral fragrance and a rich, golden hue.

Heat the olive oil in a large paella or other heavy-bottomed pan over medium-high heat. While the oil is heating, cut the pork shoulder into bite-sized chunks, then add the pork pieces to the oil and sauté until they are golden brown with a nice, even sear on both sides, about 5 to 6 minutes.

Leave the pork in pan and add the onions, garlic, and peppers. Sauté the mixture for about 2 minutes, until the onions are translucent and garlic is fragrant. Add the rice, chicken stock and saffron threads to the mixture, stir to combine, and bring it to a boil. Finally, add the shrimp, mussels, chorizo, salt and pepper. Cover the paella and lower the heat to medium-low. Let the paella simmer for 20 to 25 minutes, until the rice is cooked through and tender, and the meat and shellfish are also cooked through. Note: The mussel shells will begin to pop open as the insides finish cooking, so look for that cue. Stir in the peas and mix well to combine. Serve the paella straight from the pan, allowing each guest to ladle out their own servings.

BEVERAGE SUGGESTION

Paella pairs beautifully with a vibrant Spanish Garnacha (Grenache). Garnacha's bright red fruit and subtle spice complement the smoky pork and sweet piquillos.

Veracruz Spiced Rice

with Seafood, Tomatoes & Garlic

Arroz a la Tumbada is a vibrant and hearty Mexican seafood rice dish from the state of Veracruz that brings together the flavors of the ocean with aromatic spices. This one-pan recipe features tender rice cooked in a flavorful mix of fish stock and clam juice, infused with cumin, paprika, oregano, and a hint of chili powder. The dish is loaded with a variety of seafood, including shrimp, fish fillets, and squid, making it a delightful and satisfying meal. Topped with fresh cilantro and served with lime wedges for a zesty finish, it is a great way to bring the tastes of the sea to your table.

Serves 4

2 tablespoons extra-virgin olive oil
1 yellow onion, peeled and medium-chopped
2 cloves garlic, peeled and minced
1 large chopped tomato or 1 (8-ounce) can diced tomatoes
1½ cups rinsed rice
1½ cups fish stock or water
1 cup clam juice
1 teaspoon ground paprika
1 teaspoon ground cumin
1 teaspoon dried oregano
½ teaspoon chili powder
½ teaspoon kosher salt
½ teaspoon fresh cracked black pepper
1 pound mixed, cleaned and deveined seafood, such as shrimp, fish fillets, and squid rings
2 tablespoons chopped fresh cilantro leaves
1 sliced lime

Veracruz Meets Valencia

A Tale of Two Rices

While the vibrant, coastal flavors of Veracruz and the rich, time-honored traditions of Valencia may seem worlds apart, both culinary cultures share a deep love for seafood and rice. In Spain, paella is a beloved national dish, originating in the Valencia region, where saffron-infused rice meets an array of fresh seafood and savory meats. The rice, typically short-grain Bomba, absorbs the rich flavors of the stock and becomes tender yet firm, creating the perfect base for this iconic dish. On the other hand, Veracruz, located along Mexico's Gulf Coast, offers a distinct culinary identity, with rice often paired with the bold, tangy flavors of tomatoes, garlic, and citrus. My Veracruz Spiced Rice brings together these zesty notes, accompanied by shrimp, mussels, or other local seafood. While both dishes feature rice as their backbone, the difference lies in the flavors: paella leans on the earthiness of saffron and the smokiness of chorizo, while Veracruz rice celebrates the brightness of lime and the heat of chiles. Despite their differences, both are a delicious testament to the ability of seafood and rice to unite in a harmony of flavors, each reflecting the cultural essence of its region.

Heat the olive oil in a large skillet or pot over medium heat. Add the onion and cook until softened, about 3 minutes. Add the garlic and tomatoes and cook for another 2 minutes, until the tomato softens. Stir in the rice and cook for 2 to 3 minutes, allowing it to toast slightly.

Pour in the fish stock and clam juice and bring the mixture to a boil. Add the paprika, cumin, oregano, chili powder, salt, and pepper. Stir to combine. Lower the heat, cover, and simmer for 15 minutes, or until the rice is almost tender and most of the liquid has absorbed.

Add the seafood to the pot, mixing gently. Cover again and cook for 5 to 7 more minutes until the seafood is cooked through and the rice is tender. Stir in cilantro and adjust seasoning with salt and pepper to taste. Serve with lime wedges on the side for squeezing over the dish.

BEVERAGE SUGGESTION

Veracruz spiced rice is an excellent match with a Michelada, a classic Mexican beer cocktail made with light beer, lime juice, hot sauce, and tomato or clamato juice. The Michelada's tangy, spicy, and savory profile mirrors the bold flavors of the dish while the carbonation and lime refresh the palate between bites.

PASTAS & RISOTTOS

Pasta and risotto may be Old World staples, but for me, they're a blank canvas for bold flavor and seasonal inspiration. I love taking these comforting classics and giving them a modern spin—think spring pea ravioli with asparagus pesto, or squid ink pasta tangled with white wine–poached seafood and a hit of saffron cream. There's something deeply soothing about a bowl of noodles or a creamy risotto—nourishing, familiar, and endlessly versatile. I lean into that coziness, but always with a twist: risotto flambéed in cognac with double scampi, scallops nestled into spinach riso with smoky piquillo-almond butter, even a pasta salad punched up with homemade pecorino pesto. Whether the inspiration comes from the Gulf, the garden, or the Italian countryside, these recipes are designed to surprise, satisfy, and bring you back for another bite.

Mascarpone & Spring Pea Ravioli

with Asparagus Pesto

This recipe is a love letter to spring. Sweet English peas, creamy mascarpone, and a bright, basil-kissed asparagus pesto come together in delicate ravioli that are as fun to make as they are to eat. The flavors are fresh and light, but still indulgent—perfect for a weekend lunch in the sunshine or a dinner that feels like a little celebration. Making pasta from scratch might seem ambitious, but it's a surprisingly soothing process (and a great excuse to get your hands messy). Serve the ravioli simply, with a generous spoonful of the pesto and maybe a glass of something crisp—you've earned it.

Serves 8

Asparagus Pesto

Makes 3 cups

1 pound asparagus
½ cup packed coarsely chopped fresh basil leaves
2 tablespoons toasted pine nuts
1 tablespoon minced garlic
½ teaspoon kosher salt, divided, more as needed
¼ teaspoon fresh cracked black pepper, more as needed
1 cup extra-virgin olive oil, more to taste
½ cup freshly grated Parmigiano-Reggiano cheese, plus additional for serving

Mascarpone & Spring Pea Ravioli

DOUGH

2 cups all-purpose flour, plus more for dusting
1 teaspoon kosher salt

3 large eggs, plus 1 for egg wash
2 tablespoons extra-virgin olive oil, divided, plus more for finishing
Cornmeal, for dusting

FILLING

2 cups mascarpone cheese
2 cups blanched English peas
1/8 teaspoon kosher salt
1/8 teaspoon fresh cracked black pepper
1 teaspoon peeled, chopped, and sautéed garlic

To make the Asparagus Pesto: Bring a pot of water to a boil over medium-high heat, seasoning it with 1/4 teaspoon of the salt. Drop the asparagus spears in the water and blanch for about 2 to 3 minutes, until they brighten in color, but are still crisp-tender. Drain and rinse with cold water to stop them from cooking any more. Cut the cooked asparagus spears into thirds. Add the trimmed asparagus, plus the basil, pine nuts, garlic, the other 1/4 teaspoon salt and all the pepper to a high-powered blender or food processor fitted with a blade attachment. Note: Keep in mind you will add cheese later, so don't add any more salt at this point. Turn on the machine and slowly add the cup of olive oil with the motor running. The sauce has enough oil once it is the consistency of mayonnaise. Once you reach this texture, pulse in the Parmigiano-Reggiano. Thin with water, if necessary, to achieve a slick, saucy pesto. Taste and add more salt and pepper, if needed. Scrape into a bowl or jar, cover, and refrigerate until needed. The pesto can be prepped up to 3 days in advance, stored in an airtight container in the refrigerator; stir or shake well before using.

To make the pasta dough: Add the flour and salt to a bowl of an electric mixer fitted with a dough hook. Add the 3 eggs, 1 at a time, and continue to mix. Drizzle in 1 tablespoon of the olive oil and continue to mix until a ball forms. Note: If you don't have an electric mixer, combine the flour and salt on a flat work surface; shape into a mound and make a well in the center. Add the eggs and 1 tablespoon of the olive oil to the well and lightly beat with a fork. Gradually draw in the flour from the inside wall of the well in a circular motion. Use 1 hand for mixing and the other to protect the outer wall. Continue to incorporate all the flour until it forms a ball.

Sprinkle some flour on a work surface. Knead and fold the dough until it's elastic and smooth; this should take about 10 minutes. Brush the surface with the remaining olive oil and wrap the dough in plastic wrap; let rest at room temperature for about 30 minutes to allow the gluten to relax.

While the pasta is resting, prepare the filling: Combine the mascarpone, peas, salt, pepper and sautéed garlic in a medium-sized mixing bowl. Stir to incorporate.

Assemble the ravioli: Cut the ball of dough in half, then cover the piece you are not immediately using with plastic wrap to prevent it from drying out. Dust the counter and the dough with a little flour. Press the dough into a rectangle and roll it through a pasta machine, 2 or 3 times, at the thickest setting. Note: On most pasta machines, this will be a 1. Pull and stretch the sheet of dough with the palm of your hand as it emerges from the rollers. Reduce the setting to the next notch, usually a 2, then crank the dough through again, 2 or 3 times. Continue tightening until the machine is at the narrowest setting; the dough should be paper-thin, about 1/8-inch thick. Repeat the process with the other half of the dough. Dust the sheets of dough with flour as needed.

Beat 1 egg with 1 tablespoon of water to make an egg wash. Dust the counter and 1 sheet of pasta with flour, then brush the top surface of the pasta sheet with the egg wash, which acts as a glue. Drop tablespoons of the filling on 1/2 of the pasta sheet, about 2-inches apart. Fold the other 1/2 over the filling like a blanket. With an espresso cup or fingers, gently press out air pockets around each mound of filling. Use a sharp knife or ravioli cutter to cut each pillow into squares or circles, as desired and crimp the 4 edges with the tins of a fork to make a tight seal. Dust the ravioli and a sheet pan with cornmeal to prevent the pasta from sticking and lay them out to dry slightly while assembling the rest. Repeat with the other sheet of dough and the rest of the filling.

More than a Dessert Darling
Mascarpone's Savory Side

Smooth, rich, and subtly sweet, mascarpone is often known as the star of tiramisu—but it's just as powerful in savory dishes. This luxurious Italian cream cheese is made by curdling cream with acid, resulting in a soft, spreadable texture and a mild flavor that blends effortlessly with herbs, vegetables, and delicate pastas. In ravioli, mascarpone creates an ultra-silky filling that doesn't overpower spring ingredients like peas or asparagus—it enhances them. When folded into warm pasta or risotto, it adds creaminess without the need for a heavy sauce. For best results, use mascarpone at room temperature and mix it gently with other ingredients to preserve its smooth texture. It also makes a luscious finishing touch stirred into hot dishes just before serving, where it melts into a velvety cloak.

Place a pot of well salted water over medium-high heat and bring to a boil. Cook the ravioli for 4 minutes, working in batches as needed to not overcrowd the pot; they'll float to the top when ready. Lift the ravioli from water with a large strainer or slotted spoon.

To serve, place the ravioli in a large pasta or serving bowl, and spoon over the Asparagus Pesto, tossing lightly to coat the ravioli. Sprinkle over additional Parmigiano-Reggiano cheese, more fresh cracked black pepper, and a swirl of olive oil, as desired. Serve immediately.

BEVERAGE SUGGESTION

This ravioli recipe pairs nicely with an Austrian Grüner Veltliner or a dry Italian white like Soave or Verdicchio. These wines offer crisp acidity, subtle green notes, and a touch of minerality that highlight the freshness of the peas and asparagus while balancing the rich creaminess of the mascarpone.

Pan-Seared Chicken & Pasta Salad

with Homemade Pecorino Pesto

This bright, herb-packed pasta salad is the kind of dish that earns a permanent spot in your warm-weather rotation—hearty enough to be a main, fresh enough to feel picnic-worthy. Tender grilled chicken, perfectly *al dente* penne, and a bold, nutty pesto made with sharp Pecorino give it savory backbone, but the recipe leaves plenty of room for personalization. At the restaurant, I love adding a signature twist: folding in smoky roasted red or piquillo peppers, scattering crunchy toasted pepitas on top, or crumbling in a bit of queso fresco for a pop of creamy contrast.

Serves 8

Pecorino Pesto

Makes 2 cups

5 cups loosely packed fresh basil leaves
¾ cup extra-virgin olive oil
⅓ cup toasted pine nuts
1 clove garlic, peeled and grated
¼ cup grated Parmigiano-Reggiano cheese
¼ cup grated Pecorino Sardo or Romano cheese
⅛ teaspoon kosher salt, more to taste

Pan-Seared Chicken & Pasta Salad

1 pound dried penne pasta
2 tablespoons, plus ¼ teaspoon, kosher salt, more to taste
2 pounds skinless chicken breasts

¼ teaspoon fresh cracked black pepper, more to taste
3 tablespoons extra-virgin olive oil

To make the Pecorino Pesto: Add the basil leaves, olive oil, pine nuts, and garlic to a high-powered blender or food processor fitted with a blade attachment. Pulse until a paste forms, stopping often to push down the basil to ensure it gets finely chopped. Add the cheeses and pulse until well combined and smooth. Stir in the salt, and taste for seasoning, adding more if desired. Set pesto aside in a bowl. The pesto can be prepared up to 2 to 3 days in advance. Store in an airtight container in the refrigerator; allow to come to room temperature and give the pesto a good stir to redistribute the oil before use.

Bring a large pot of water to a boil over medium-high heat, seasoning it well with 2 tablespoons of the kosher salt. Cook pasta until *al dente*—tender, but still with some bite to it—about 7 to 8 minutes, then drain and rinse until cold.

Meanwhile, heat a large pan over medium heat. Pat the chicken dry then season with the remaining ¼ teaspoon salt and the pepper on both sides. Sear the chicken in olive oil until golden brown and cooked through, about 3 minutes per side. Transfer the chicken to a cutting board, allow to rest for 2 to 3 minutes, and then cut into thin strips.

Add the pasta, sliced chicken, and half of the Pecorino Pesto to a large bowl. Mix well and, if needed, add more of the pesto to get the consistency just right. Taste test and make final adjustments to salt and pepper, if desired. The salad can be eaten right away or chilled for a few hours before serving.

BEVERAGE SUGGESTION

Pan-seared chicken and pasta salad with homemade Pecorino pesto pairs beautifully with a crisp, medium-bodied Italian Vermentino. This wine offers bright acidity and subtle herbal and citrus notes that complement the salty, nutty Pecorino and the richness of the chicken without overpowering the fresh, vibrant pesto.

Squid Ink Pasta with White Wine–Kissed Seafood

and Saffron Cream Sauce

Luxurious, aromatic, indulgent, delicate—this striking main dish hits all the high notes. The black strands of squid ink pasta provide a visually stunning contrast to the succulent shrimp, scallops, and calamari, while the saffron cream sauce adds a fragrant, golden touch, enhancing the seafood without overpowering it. Squid ink pasta, incidentally, is readily available to order online and it's worth a purchase for this show-stopping presentation. However, you can alternatively substitute in your favorite pasta. Whether served as the centerpiece of an intimate dinner party or a quiet night in with a glass of crisp white wine, this is a dish that makes any meal feel just a little bit more magical.

Serves 4

Saffron Cream Sauce

Makes about 1 cup

¼ teaspoon saffron threads
2 tablespoons warm water
1 tablespoon unsalted butter
½ cup heavy cream
¼ cup chicken or seafood broth
⅛ teaspoon kosher salt, more to taste
⅛ teaspoon fresh cracked black pepper

Squid Ink Pasta with White Wine–Kissed Seafood

¾ pound squid ink linguine pasta
1 tablespoon extra-virgin olive oil

2 cloves garlic, peeled and minced
½ pound cleaned scallops
½ pound cleaned calamari
½ pound peeled and deveined shrimp
¼ teaspoon kosher salt, more to taste
¼ teaspoon fresh cracked black pepper, more to taste
½ cup dry white wine
1 tablespoon chopped fresh Italian flat-leaf parsley leaves
Micro Intensity Mix, for garnish, optional
Grated Parmigiano-Reggiano cheese, for serving

To make the Saffron Cream Sauce: Add the saffron threads to a small bowl and pour over the warm water. Allow the saffron to steep in the water for about 5 minutes. Add the butter to a medium-size saucepan over medium heat and allow it to melt. Once melted, add the heavy cream and broth. Stir in the saffron infusion, both the water and threads, and bring the mixture to a simmer. Let it cook for about 5 to 7 minutes, until the sauce slightly thickens and coats the back of a spoon. Season with the salt and pepper, taste for seasoning, and add more, if desired. Keep warm until ready to toss with the pasta. Any leftover sauce will keep for 2 to 3 days, stored in an airtight container in the refrigerator.

Bring a large pot of well-salted water to a boil over medium heat. Cook the squid ink pasta according to package instructions, usually about 7 to 10 minutes, until *al dente*, with some bite left to it. Drain, reserving about 1 cup of pasta water for later.

Heat the olive oil in a large skillet over medium-high heat. Add the garlic and sauté for 1 minute, until fragrant.

Slice the scallops into halves if on the larger size and slice the calamari into thin rings. Add the scallops, calamari, and shrimp to the skillet and cook for 3 to 4 minutes, turning occasionally, until the seafood is cooked through and opaque. Season with the salt and pepper.

Add the white wine to the skillet, letting it simmer for 1 to 2 minutes to reduce slightly. Remove the seafood from heat and stir in the fresh parsley. Add the cooked squid ink pasta to the skillet with the seafood and toss gently to coat in the wine and garlic mixture. If the pasta seems dry, add a bit of the reserved pasta water to help loosen it up.

Pour the Saffron Cream Sauce over the pasta and seafood, tossing again until everything is evenly coated. Serve immediately in pasta bowls, garnished with micro greens, if using, and freshly grated Parmigiano-Reggiano cheese on the side.

BEVERAGE SUGGESTION

Squid ink pasta with white wine–infused seafood and saffron cream sauce pairs beautifully with a French Chablis. Chablis offers crisp minerality and acidity that cut through the saffron cream and complement the pasta's briny depth.

Double Scampi-Infused Risotto

with Asparagus & Cognac Flambé

This risotto is a showstopper—luxurious, layered, and just a little bit theatrical. Built on a homemade scampi shell broth that deepens the dish with briny complexity, it doubles down on flavor by finishing with a quick cognac flambé of tender scampi and crisp asparagus tips. The arborio rice absorbs every bit of that rich essence, creating a dish that feels both indulgent and fresh. At its heart, this is a soulful, seafood-forward risotto with flair—comfort food dressed for a night out.

Serves 4

12 to 16 large langoustine or other shell-on shrimp scampi
6 cups water
1 large carrot, peeled and chopped
1 white onion, peeled and chopped, divided
1 bay leaf
1 tablespoon whole black peppercorns
1/8 teaspoon kosher salt
20 asparagus spears
4 tablespoons extra-virgin olive oil, divided
1 cup Arborio rice
1/2 cup dry white wine
1 tablespoon cognac
1 tablespoon unsalted butter
2 tablespoons grated Parmigiano-Reggiano cheese
1/2 teaspoon fresh cracked black pepper

First, prep the scampi-infused broth: Peel and clean the scampi, cutting each one in half lengthwise. Refrigerate the scampi until ready to use. Next, rinse the shells (and

Flame, Flavor, Finish

Cooking with Cognac

Cognac isn't just for sipping by the fire—it's a brilliant tool for deepening flavor in savory dishes, especially those featuring seafood or cream. This French brandy is aged in oak barrels, which gives it warm, layered notes of dried fruit, spice, and vanilla. When used in cooking—particularly as a flambé—it does two things: it adds rich complexity and burns off quickly, leaving behind just the essence of its elegant aroma. In risotto, flambéing cognac with seafood helps lift and integrate the briny, buttery notes of shellfish while balancing the creaminess of the rice. To flambé safely, always remove the pan from direct heat before adding the alcohol, then carefully ignite with a long match or lighter, letting the flames die out naturally. No flambé? No problem. A splash stirred in at the very end brings the depth without the drama.

heads if using langoustines). Place the shells in a large pot over medium-high heat with the water, the chopped carrot, ½ of the chopped onion, bay leaf, and peppercorns. Add the salt and let boil for 30 minutes. Strain out the solids and transfer the strained broth back to the pot and keep warm over low heat.

Discard the tough ends of the asparagus and cut the tips off. Put the tips aside, reserving those for later, and cut the rest of the asparagus stalks into ½-inch pieces. Add 2 tablespoons of the olive oil to a large sauté pan over medium heat. Once the oil is shimmering, add the remaining ½ of the onions, and sauté until soft, about 3 to 4 minutes. Stir in the asparagus stalk pieces and the rice, making sure both are nicely coated with the oil. Pour in the white wine and bring to a simmer, allowing the mixture to cook 2 to 3 minutes until the wine is almost evaporated. Add in 2 cups of the reserved scampi broth and stir well, letting the risotto simmer for another 5 to 8 minutes, or until most of the liquid has been absorbed. Add another 2 cups of broth and stir, repeating the process, until the rice is tender and cooked through. Note: If you want a creamier risotto, add more broth. You may or may not use all the reserved broth.

When the risotto is almost ready, heat the other 2 tablespoons olive oil in another pan over medium-high heat. Once the oil is shimmering, sauté both the reserved scampi and asparagus tips until heated through, about 2 minutes. Carefully pour over the cognac and flambé for about 1 minute, shaking the pan vigorously, until the cognac is evaporated. Remove from the heat.

Add the asparagus and scampi to the pot of risotto, tossing well to combine. Add the butter and cheese and allow the butter to melt into risotto before removing from the heat. Serve immediately with a generous sprinkle of black pepper and more grated Parmigiano-Reggiano cheese, if desired.

BEVERAGE SUGGESTION

This risotto with asparagus and cognac flambé is delicious with a white Burgundy (like a Meursault) or a Champagne Blanc de Blancs. The Burgundy's rich texture and layered minerality match the depth of the seafood and cognac while its acidity balances the creaminess. The Champagne's crisp bubbles and citrus notes, meanwhile, lift the richness and echo the elegance of the dish.

Pan-Seared Scallops over Spinach Riso Pasta

with Marcona Almond–Piquillo Butter Sauce

Golden, pan-seared scallops steal the spotlight in this vibrant and satisfying dish, nestled atop a bed of tender riso pasta tossed with wilted spinach and aromatic shallots. What sets it apart is the velvety butter sauce—infused with sweet piquillo peppers and the irresistible crunch of Marcona almonds—that drape over the scallops in a final flourish. The interplay of textures and bold flavors makes this recipe a standout for a special evening, yet it's also simple enough to master on a weeknight.

Serves 4

Marcona Almond–Piquillo Butter Sauce

Makes about 2 cups

½ cup unsalted butter
½ cup diced piquillo peppers
¼ cup chopped toasted Marcona almonds
½ cup dry white wine
⅛ teaspoon kosher salt, more to taste
⅛ teaspoon fresh cracked black pepper, more to taste

Spinach Riso Pasta

Makes 4 cups

2 cups riso or orzo pasta
1 tablespoon extra-virgin olive oil
1 small shallot, peeled and finely diced
2 cloves garlic, peeled and crushed
2 cups cleaned fresh spinach leaves

¼ teaspoon kosher salt, more for salting the pasta water and to taste
¼ teaspoon fresh cracked black pepper, more to taste

Pan-Seared Scallops

12 (U-10) cleaned scallops
¼ teaspoon kosher salt, more to taste
¼ teaspoon fresh cracked black pepper, more to taste
2 tablespoons extra-virgin olive oil
Micro Shiso Red, for garnish, optional

To make the Marcona Almond-Piquillo Butter Sauce: Add the butter, diced piquillo peppers, and Marcona almonds to a sauté pan and turn the heat to high, allowing the butter to melt. Once the butter is melted, pour in the white wine. Bring the mixture to a simmer and cook until the sauce reduces and thickens to a rich consistency, about 5 minutes. Season with the salt and pepper, taste for seasoning, and add more, if desired. Turn the heat down to very low and reserve on the stove until ready for use.

To make the Spinach Riso Pasta: Bring a pot of well-salted water to a boil over medium-high heat. Once boiling, drop in the pasta and cook until al dente, chewy with some bite left, about 4 to 6 minutes. Drain and set aside. Heat the olive oil in a nonstick sauté pan over medium heat. Once the oil is shimmering, add the shallots and garlic, and cook for 2 to 3 minutes, until fragrant. Add the spinach and cook until it wilts down, about 1 minute. Stir in the cooked riso pasta and season with the salt and pepper. Taste for seasoning and adjust, if desired. Turn the heat to very low and allow to sit on the stove while you prepare the scallops.

Season the scallops with the salt and pepper and allow them to sit out at room temperature for a few minutes so they aren't too cold when they hit the pan. Heat the oil in a sauté pan over medium-high heat until very hot and shimmering. Add the scallops one by one, browning them on one side. Once they are golden, flip the scallops and reduce the heat to low. Cook for an additional 2 to 3 minutes, or until the scallops are cooked through.

A Simple Primer
Cleaning Scallops

Scallops are prized for their delicate texture and sweet, briny flavor—but to get the most from them, a quick bit of prep is essential. The good news? Cleaning them is fast and easy. Start by locating the side muscle, a small, slightly tougher flap attached to the edge of each scallop. It's perfectly safe to eat, but it can be a bit chewy, so most chefs prefer to remove it. Simply pinch it between your fingers and gently pull it away—it should release cleanly. Give the scallops a quick rinse under cold water, just enough to remove any residual sand or grit, then thoroughly pat them dry with a paper towel. This last step is key: a dry scallop will sear much more effectively, developing that crisp, golden crust you're after. If you're working with "wet" scallops (those treated with a preservative solution), a brief soak in cold water with a splash of lemon juice or milk can help remove any off flavors. Still, when possible, opt for "dry" scallops, which are untreated and offer the best flavor and texture for high-heat cooking. A bit of careful prep goes a long way—and ensures your scallops shine exactly as they should.

To assemble the dish, spoon a portion of the Spinach Riso Pasta on each plate, then top with 3 seared scallops each. Spoon the Marcona Almond–Piquillo Butter Sauce over the scallops and riso. Garnish with the micro greens, if using, and serve immediately.

BEVERAGE SUGGESTION

Pan-seared scallops and a white Spanish Rioja (Viura-based) are a match made in heaven. The white Rioja's subtle oak, nuttiness, and round texture echo the richness of the almond-piquillo butter.

BIRDS

Feathered fare takes flight in this chapter, where chicken, duck, and quail are coaxed into their most soulful forms. In these recipes, I lean into the comfort food traditions I grew up with and still cook today—whether it's a slow-braised coq au vin, smoky deviled eggs with a spicy crunch, or the kind of chicken soup that feels like a warm hug. But comfort doesn't have to mean conventional. This is continental cooking with a Texas heart: French technique, Mexican spice, a touch of Asian flair—all mingling in ways that feel both familiar and new. From tea-smoked duck tucked into crispy pancakes to roulades wrapped in pine nut mole, I love how these birds carry bold flavors across borders. Whether I'm chasing backyard barbecue vibes or aiming for candlelit dinner party polish, these dishes always deliver.

Black Tea–Smoked Duck Breasts

with Crispy Asian Pancakes

This dish is all about contrast—where smoky meets crispy, and bold flavor meets delicate texture. Inspired by classic Chinese tea-smoking techniques, the duck breasts are first seared to render their rich skin, then gently infused with the earthy aroma of black tea, cinnamon, and star anise. Paired with homemade crispy pancakes that are surprisingly simple to make, each bite becomes a perfect little package of savory, spiced goodness. It's a recipe that feels special but doesn't require a restaurant kitchen—just a bit of patience, attention to detail, and a willingness to lean into the process.

Serves 2

Crispy Asian Pancakes

Makes 12 pancakes

2 cups all-purpose flour, more for kneading
½ teaspoon kosher salt
¾ cup boiling water
1 tablespoon vegetable oil

Black Tea–Smoked Duck Breasts

2 boneless, skin-on duck breasts
¼ teaspoon kosher salt
¼ teaspoon fresh cracked black pepper
1 tablespoon extra-virgin olive oil
2 tablespoons black tea leaves
2 tablespoons long-grain white rice
1 tablespoon sugar

1 tablespoon sesame seeds
1 whole cinnamon stick
1 star anise
Fresh chopped cilantro or parsley leaves, for garnish
Soy sauce or hoisin sauce, for serving
Cooked jasmine rice, for serving, optional

To make the Crispy Asian Pancakes: Add the flour and salt to a large bowl. Gradually pour the boiling water into the flour mixture, stirring well as you go along. Once a dough begins to form and pull away from the edges of the bowl, remove the dough to a lightly floured cutting board or work surface. Knead the dough for about 5 minutes, flipping it over a few times and adding more flour, as needed, to avoid sticking, until it is smooth and elastic. Place the dough back into the mixing bowl and cover with a damp cloth. Allow to rest for 30 minutes.

After resting, divide the dough into 12 equal portions and roll each ball into a thin circle, about 6 inches in diameter, on a lightly floured surface. Brush a thin layer of vegetable oil on one side of each pancake and then stack them on a plastic wrap-lined plate with the oiled sides facing each other to prevent sticking.

Heat a non-stick skillet or pan over medium-high heat. Place the pancakes in the skillet one at a time and cook each side for about 1 to 2 minutes, flipping once or twice, until the pancake is slightly golden and crispy. Remove and allow to cool for a few minutes before using. These are best made fresh, but if you'd like to prep them in advance, wrap tightly in plastic wrap and refrigerate up to 1 day in advance. Lightly reheat in a skillet with some oil to ensure they still have a crispy texture once served.

To begin the duck breasts, place the breasts on a plastic cutting board and lightly score the skin of the duck breasts in a crisscross pattern using a sharp knife, being careful not to cut into the meat. Sprinkle both sides with of the breasts with the salt and pepper.

Heat a large skillet over medium-high heat. Add the olive oil and once shimmering, place the duck breasts skin-side down in the oil. Sear the duck breasts for about 6 to 8 minutes or until the skin is crispy and golden brown. Flip the duck breasts and cook the other side for about 3 to 4 minutes, until the internal temperature reaches 130-135°F for medium-rare. Remove the duck breasts from the skillet and set them aside to rest while you prep the smoke mixture.

Add the black tea leaves, rices, sugar, sesame seeds, cinnamon stick, and star anise to a small bowl. Line a wok or a deep pan with aluminum foil. Spread the tea-smoking mixture evenly in the bottom of the wok. Place a wire rack or a steaming rack inside the wok, above the smoking mixture. Note: This will create a makeshift "smoking tray." If you don't have a wok, you can simply use a large pot with a lid and a rack that fits inside.

Put the duck breasts on the rack, skin-side up. Cover the wok with the lid, or some foil, to trap the smoke inside. Heat the wok over medium heat until you begin to see smoke rising from the mixture. Once smoking, reduce the heat to low and let the duck breasts smoke for about 10 to 15 minutes. For a stronger smoky flavor, you can let it smoke for a bit longer.

Remove the duck breasts and let them rest for a few minutes. Slice the duck against the grain.

The Art of Tea-Smoking

Infusing Duck with Depth

Smoking meat is an ancient cooking technique that imparts deep, complex flavors by exposing food to the aromatic smoke of burning wood or herbs. While many might think of smoky flavors coming solely from wood chips, tea-smoking is a lesser-known method that offers a nuanced, sophisticated smokiness. In this recipe, black tea—known for its bold, tannic flavor—becomes the base for the smoking mixture, alongside rice and sugar, which help to create the ideal environment. The duck breasts absorb the fragrant smoke, giving them a distinct, delicate depth that pairs beautifully with crispy pancakes and sweet, spicy plum sauce. Tea-smoking is also incredibly versatile; you can experiment with different teas (like oolong or green) to vary the profile. It's important to allow the duck to rest after smoking to fully absorb the flavors. The result? A perfect balance of rich, tender meat with a smoky, aromatic finish.

Scatter fresh herbs over the duck, if desired, and serve with Crispy Asian Pancakes, soy or hoisin sauce, and rice, if using, on the side.

BEVERAGE SUGGESTION

Black tea–smoked duck breasts and a Japanese sake like a dry Junmai or a Ginjo is my go-to combination. The clean, slightly fruity, and umami-rich profile of sake complements the smoky richness of the duck and the delicate pancakes, enhancing the dish's savory, sweet and aromatic Asian flavors.

Chicken Fricassée

with Mushrooms, Smoked Bacon & Potatoes

Chicken Fricassée is a comforting and elegant French dish that blends the best of a sauté and a stew. It's known for its creamy white sauce and tender chicken, often complemented with mushrooms, onions, and sometimes white wine. Here, I've added chopped smoked bacon for an additional savory note. I love making this dish on a cold day, served with a slice of toasted rustic bread rubbed with garlic to sop up all the creamy juices.

Serves 4

1 (3- to 4-pound) whole chicken
4 tablespoons all-purpose flour, divided
½ teaspoon kosher salt, more for seasoning
½ teaspoon fresh cracked black pepper, more for seasoning
1 cup unsalted butter
½ pound applewood smoked bacon, diced
1 yellow onion, peeled and diced
1 clove garlic, peeled and finely chopped
1 cup dry white wine
½ teaspoon ground nutmeg
2 cups water
4 Yukon Gold or other small potatoes, quartered
4 cups sliced white button mushrooms
2 tablespoons heavy cream
Rustic bread, for serving

Pat the chicken dry with a paper towel, then use a very sharp knife to break the chicken down into 8 pieces: 2 breasts, 2 thighs, 2 drumsticks, and 2 wings. Note: If necessary, see the sidebar here for more details on how to break down a chicken.

Place 3 tablespoons of the flour on a large plate or in a baking dish and season with the salt and pepper, mixing to combine. Dredge all the chicken pieces in the flour, coating all sides and tapping off any excess flour.

Melt the butter in a large heavy bottomed pot or Dutch oven over medium-high heat. Brown the chicken pieces in the butter until they boast a nice, golden-brown exterior. Add the diced bacon and diced yellow onion and cook for 5 to 6 minutes, until the bacon is crispy and rendered and the onions are tender. Add the garlic and cook until fragrant, 1 additional minute. Sprinkle with remaining 1 tablespoon flour, stirring to incorporate, and allow the flour to cook for 1 to 2 minutes. Add the white wine and bring to a simmer. Cook for 5 to 6 minutes, or until the wine is reduced by half. Add the nutmeg, and season with additional salt and pepper, if desired. Add the water and the potatoes, and bring to a simmer, continuing to simmer gently for about 45 minutes, or until the chicken is cooked through and the sauce has thickened.

Add the mushrooms and stir in the cream. Let cook for another 5 minutes, until the mushrooms are tender. Check for seasoning and adjust, as needed. Serve warm with a side of toasted bread for dunking.

BEVERAGE SUGGESTION

Chicken fricassée with mushrooms, smoked bacon, and potatoes pairs nicely with a white Burgundy (such as Meursault or Pouilly-Fuissé). The white Burgundy's creamy texture and subtle oak harmonize with the richness of the fricassée.

Breaking It Down

1 Bird, 8 Perfect Portions

I love to use whole chickens in my cooking. Not only do they help bring big flavor to the table, but they are also extremely economical to purchase and help to reduce food waste by utilizing the entire bird. Don't be intimidated by the butchering; here, I've given you a step-by-step guide to easily break down this beautiful bird. You'll be a pro in no time:

- First, place the chicken on a plastic cutting board, breast side up.
- Run a very sharp knife down the center of the chicken and slice down, splitting it in two.
- Pull a wing out and remove the first two joint sections by cutting through the socket.
- Then, with one of the legs in hand, run your knife between the breast and leg to cut the skin. Continue to pull the leg while cutting and follow through to the joint and cut through.
- Once the leg is removed, pull the thigh and separate it from the socket.
- Finally, to remove the breast, run the knife from the top of the chicken to the bottom while making multiple passes down through the wishbone and breastplate and all the way to the wing bone. Cut the breast from the wing bone.
- Repeat the entire process with the other half of chicken; you should then have 2 breasts, 2 thighs, 2 drumsticks, and 2 wings, all ready and raring to go.

Cremini Mushroom–Filled Chicken Roulades

with Pine Nut Mole

This creative dish combines tender, rolled chicken with a rich and nutty mole sauce. The roulade is made by flattening chicken breast, filling it with ingredients like shallots, goat cheese, mushrooms, and hoja santa, then rolling and searing it to achieve a golden crust before finishing in the oven. Hoja santa, if you're not familiar, is a culinary herb native to Mexico and South America. Its leaves are heart-shaped, velvety, and can be used as an edible wrapper or to flavor dishes like this one. You can often find it at Mexican food specialty stores, but if not, you could alternatively use Mexican tarragon or even French tarragon. The pine nut mole, meanwhile, is a unique twist on traditional mole sauces, featuring toasted pine nuts blended with garlic, onions, and just a touch of cream. This results in a smooth, slightly sweet, and deeply flavorful sauce. Served with a side of rice, roasted vegetables, or a fresh herb salad, this dish offers a balance of bold flavors, tender textures, and a visually striking presentation.

Serves 4

Pine Nut Mole

Makes 1½ cups

2 tablespoons unsalted butter
1 yellow onion, peeled and chopped
2 Anaheim chiles, seeded and diced
1 cup pine nuts, plus more for garnish
2 cups chicken broth or stock
¼ teaspoon kosher salt, more to taste
¼ teaspoon fresh cracked black pepper, more to taste

1 teaspoon fresh thyme leaves
2 to 3 tablespoons heavy cream, optional

Cremini Mushroom–Filled Chicken Roulades

2 tablespoons olive oil, divided
2 cups sliced cremini mushrooms
1 medium shallot, peeled and minced
1 teaspoon peeled and minced garlic
2 teaspoons kosher salt, divided
2 teaspoons fresh-cracked black pepper, divided
½ teaspoon fresh thyme leaves
1 cup crumbled goat cheese
⅓ cup finely chopped hoja santa
4 boneless, skinless chicken breasts
1 tablespoon unsalted butter
Edible marigold flowers, for garnish, optional

To make the Pine Nut Mole: Melt the butter in a skillet over medium heat. Add the onion and chiles and cook until the onions are translucent, scraping up the bits at the bottom of the pan, 8 to 10 minutes. Stir in the pine nuts and toast for 1 to 2 minutes, stirring to prevent burning. Add the chicken stock, salt, pepper, and thyme, and bring to a boil. Lower the heat and simmer until thickened and reduced, about 10 minutes. For a creamier sauce, whisk in the cream. Remove from the heat and transfer to a blender. Purée until smooth, then adjust seasoning. The mole can be made 2 to 3 days ahead and refrigerated.

To prepare the roulades: Heat 1 tablespoon oil in a skillet over medium heat until shimmering. Add the mushrooms and shallot and cook for 5 to 6 minutes, until the mushrooms release their liquid and begin to brown. Stir in the garlic and cook for 1 minute. Add 1 teaspoon of salt and pepper, plus the thyme. Remove from the heat, strain excess liquid (reserve for a pan sauce, if desired), and transfer solids to a bowl. Mix in the goat cheese and hoja santa. Set aside.

Halve the chicken breasts horizontally, keeping one side attached and open like a book. Place between plastic wrap and pound to 1/4-inch thickness. Spread the filling along the lower third of each breast, leaving a 1/2-inch border. Roll tightly, season with the remaining salt and pepper, and wrap each roulade in plastic wrap.

Bring a large pot of water to a boil. Unwrap the roulades and carefully drop into the pot. Poach until cooked through, about 10 minutes. Remove with a slotted spoon.

Heat the remaining oil and butter in a large skillet over medium-high heat. When shimmering, add the roulades and brown on all sides to form a crust. Remove from the heat and rest for a few minutes.

To serve: Slice the roulades into rounds. Spoon a pool of Pine Nut Mole onto each plate, top with 3 or 4 roulade slices, and garnish with pine nuts and marigold petals, if using. Serve immediately.

BEVERAGE SUGGESTION

When enjoying these roulades with pine nut mole, try a medium-bodied Mexican red wine like a Valle de Guadalupe Nebbiolo or Garnacha. These wines offer bright red fruit, moderate tannins, and subtle earthiness that complement the umami mushrooms and rich, nutty mole.

SLOW-BRAISED COQ AU VIN

with Pearl Onions, Carrots & Mushrooms

Coq au Vin is an absolute classic—arguably one of the most iconic French dishes and a contender for the ultimate chicken dish. It's rustic yet refined, hearty yet elegant, and packed with deep, comforting flavors. One of the best things about coq au vin is how the long, slow cooking process transforms simple ingredients into something truly special. The wine infuses the chicken with richness, the bacon adds smokiness, and the aromatics create a sauce that's silky, savory, and irresistible. And while it has an air of sophistication, at its heart, it's a humble, homey dish meant to be shared; here's my take on the beloved favorite.

Serves 4

3 pounds chicken legs and thighs
2½ teaspoons kosher salt, divided, more to taste
½ teaspoon fresh cracked black pepper, more to taste
3 cups Burgundy or other hearty red wine
1 bay leaf
1 teaspoon chopped fresh thyme leaves
1 cup diced lardons, pancetta, or bacon
3 tablespoons extra-virgin olive oil
1 large yellow onion, peeled and diced
1 large carrot, peeled and diced
12 whole pearl onions, peeled
4 cups white or brown mushrooms, sliced
2 cloves garlic, peeled and minced
1 teaspoon tomato paste
1 tablespoon all-purpose flour

2 tablespoons brandy
3 tablespoons unsalted butter
Baguette bread, for serving

Season the chicken with 2¼ teaspoons of the salt and all the pepper, then combine the seasoned chicken in a large bowl with the wine, bay leaf, and thyme. Cover and refrigerate for at least 2 hours or, even better, overnight.

Add the lardons, pancetta, or bacon to a large Dutch oven or a heavy-bottomed pot with a tightfitting lid and cook over medium-low heat until fat has rendered, and lardons are golden and crisp, 10 to 15 minutes. Transfer lardons to a paper towel-lined plate using a slotted spoon, leaving the rendered fat in the pot.

Remove the chicken from the wine mixture, reserving the marinade. Pat chicken pieces with paper towels until very dry. Heat the lardon fat over medium heat until it's shimmering but not smoking. Working in batches, if necessary, add the chicken in a single layer and cook until well browned, 3 to 5 minutes per side. Note: Add the olive oil if the pot looks a little dry. Transfer chicken to a plate once it browns and reserve.

Add diced onion, carrot, pearl onions, and mushrooms and the remaining ¼ teaspoon salt to the same pot. Cook over medium heat until vegetables are lightly browned, about 8 minutes, stirring up any brown bits from the pot, and adjusting heat if necessary to prevent burning.

Stir in garlic and tomato paste and cook for 1 minute, then stir in the flour and cook for another minute. Remove from the heat, push the vegetables to one side of the pot, and pour the brandy into the empty side. Ignite the brandy with a match or lighter. Note: If you're too nervous to ignite it, just cook brandy down for 1 minute. Once the flame dies down, add reserved wine marinade, bring the mixture to a boil, and reduce halfway, to about 1½ cups. This should take about 10 to 12 minutes. Skim off any large pockets of foam that form on the surface.

Add the reserved chicken along with any accumulated juices to the pot and stir in the cooked lardons. Cover and simmer over low heat for 1 hour, turning the chicken over about halfway through. Uncover the pot and simmer for an additional 15 minutes to thicken. Taste and add more salt and pepper, as desired. Serve warm in bowls with a hunk of crusty bread alongside.

BEVERAGE SUGGESTION

Slow-braised Coq au Vin with pearl onions, carrots, and mushrooms pairs classically with a Burgundy Pinot Noir. The wine's earthy undertones, bright acidity, and delicate red fruit complement the rustic flavors of the braise, while its light body enhances the dish's depth.

Smoky-Spicy Deviled Eggs with Crispy Cracklings

and Red Chile Salsa

These deviled eggs are a bold twist on the classic appetizer. The creamy, rich egg yolk mixture is spiced up with a smoky, tangy chile de árbol salsa, which adds a fiery kick and deep flavor. The salsa is made from dried peppers, blending heat and smokiness with a hint of garlic and lime. Topped with crispy chicharrónes—yes, those irresistible fried pork skin nibbles you find in stores—these eggs are a crave-worthy combination of creamy, spicy, and crunchy, all in one bite.

Serves 6

Red Chile Salsa

Makes about 2 cups

2 cloves garlic, peeled
2 tomatoes, halved
1 small white onion, peeled and quartered
1 tablespoon extra-virgin olive oil
4 dried chile de árbol chiles, seeded
1 cup water or stock
½ cup chopped cilantro leaves
¼ teaspoon kosher salt, more to taste
¼ teaspoon fresh cracked black pepper, more to taste

Smoky-Spicy Deviled Eggs with Crispy Cracklings

6 large eggs
3 avocados
2 tablespoons finely diced red onion
½ cup seeded and finely diced tomato

FRESH
EGGS
BEST
IN
TOWN!

1 tablespoon chopped cilantro leaves
1 teaspoon lime juice
½ teaspoon minced garlic
¼ teaspoon kosher salt, more to taste
¼ teaspoon fresh cracked black pepper, more to taste
½ cup ground chicharrónes pork rind cracklings
Edible violets, for garnish, optional

To make the Red Chile Salsa: Add the garlic cloves, tomato halves, and onion quarters to a skillet over medium-high heat and lightly char the vegetables for about 10 minutes, flipping over once or twice. You want to toast them until they have some black spots on the outside and are almost cooked through. Remove them from the pan using a pair of kitchen tongs and place them in a high-powered blender or food processor fitted with the blade attachment. Allow to cool for a few minutes. Meanwhile, add olive oil to the same skillet over medium-high heat and quickly toss in the chiles, removing them as soon as they deepen in color as they burn easily. Carefully pour in the water or stock. Bring to a boil, and allow to boil for about 3 to 4 minutes. Transfer the chile liquid to the blender or processor. Add the cilantro and purée until the salsa is smooth, pulsing a few times to make sure there aren't any big chunks left behind. Season with the salt and pepper, adding more, if desired. Reserve in an airtight container until ready to use. The salsa can be prepared ahead; leftovers can also be stored in the refigerator for up to 2 weeks.

To start the deviled eggs, place the eggs in a medium-sized pot and cover with cold water by 1 inch. Bring to a boil over medium-high heat, then cover the pot and turn off the heat. Let the eggs cook, covered, for about 12 minutes. Transfer the eggs to a bowl of ice water and chill for 15 minutes.This makes the eggs easier to peel. Peel the eggs, then slice each in half. Separate the egg yolks from the whites. Reserve the whites in a bowl.

Push the egg yolks through a fine sieve into a small bowl using a small spoon. Halve the avocados and scoop out the avocado flesh into the same bowl and mash everything together until it is smooth and creamy in texture. Add the red onions, tomato, cilantro, lime juice and minced garlic. Season with salt and pepper, adding more to taste, if desired. Scoop a few tablespoons of the mix into the reserved egg whites, filling the cavities with nicely rounded portions. Sprinkle the tops with the ground cracklings.

To serve, spoon about 1 cup of the Red Chile Salsa out on a serving platter and top with the eggs, serving extra salsa alongside. Garnish with the edible flowers, if using, and serve.

BEVERAGE SUGGESTION

These deviled eggs pair perfectly with a smoked porter or hoppy IPA. The porter's roasted malt and subtle smokiness echo the smoky flavors in the dish while an IPA's bright bitterness and citrusy hop notes cut through the richness and balance the spicy heat.

Spicy Fried Chicken

with Grilled Peaches & Texas Peach-Whiskey Sauce

Golden, crispy, and bursting with flavor, this fried chicken is a true Southern delight. The rich, caramelized sweetness of grilled peaches blends seamlessly with the bold kick of Texas whiskey, creating a sauce that's both comforting and unexpected. Every bite is a balance of crunch, tenderness, and a touch of heat, making this dish a standout on any table. Whether served with warm buttermilk biscuits or a side of creamy mashed potatoes, it's a recipe that brings people together—one saucy, crispy bite at a time.

Texas Peach-Whiskey Sauce

Makes 3 cups

1 cup peach juice or purée
1 cup high-quality bourbon whiskey
1 cup veal demi-glace
¼ teaspoon kosher salt, more to taste
¼ teaspoon fresh cracked black pepper, more to taste

Spicy Fried Chicken

2 (3-pound) whole chickens
1 teaspoon kosher salt, divided, more to taste
1 teaspoon fresh cracked black pepper, divided, more to taste
1½ cups of water
2 tablespoons hot pepper sauce
3 large eggs
2 cups all-purpose flour
1 tablespoon ground cayenne pepper
1½ teaspoons garlic powder

½ teaspoon ground paprika
6 to 8 cups vegetable oil

Grilled Peaches

Makes 6 peach halves

3 ripe but still firm peaches
1 tablespoon extra-virgin olive oil
¼ teaspoon kosher salt, more to taste
¼ teaspoon fresh cracked black pepper, more to taste

To make the Texas-Peach Whiskey Sauce: Add the peach juice or purée and whiskey to a small saucepan over medium heat. Bring to a simmer and then continue to simmer until the mixture is reduced by half, about 8 to 10 minutes. Add in the demi-glace and stir to combine. Once the mixture is silky-smooth, add the salt and pepper. Taste for seasoning and add more, if desired. Set aside until ready to use. The sauce can be prepped up to 4 to 5 days in advance, stored in an airtight container in the refrigerator. Gently rewarm before using.

To make the Fried Chicken: Pat the chicken dry with a paper towel, then use a very sharp knife to break the chicken down into 8 pieces: 2 breasts, 2 thighs, 2 drumsticks, and 2 wings. Note: For pointers on breaking down a chicken, see the sidebar on page 195. Season the chicken pieces liberally with ½ teaspoon of the salt and ½ teaspoon of the pepper.

Add the water, eggs, and hot pepper sauce to a large bowl. Whisk together. Add the chicken pieces to the bowl and turn to coat well in the marinade mixture. Cover the bowl tightly with plastic wrap. Refrigerate for about 2 hours, or up to overnight, to marinate.

Add the flour, cayenne pepper, garlic powder, paprika, and the remaining ½ teaspoon salt and pepper to a large bowl. Mix to combine. Remove the chicken pieces from the marinade mixture, tapping off any excess dripping liquid and then dredge each piece of chicken in the flour mixture, then back in the egg-pepper marinade, and then back in the flour mix. Chef's note: This double flouring process will give a crispier, thicker crust after frying.

Heat the vegetable oil in a deep-fryer or large, heavy-bottomed saucepan until it is shimmering. Gently drop the chicken pieces into the hot oil, working in batches to avoid overcrowding, and fry until chicken is cooked through and golden brown on both sides, about 8 to 10 minutes for the breasts and wings, and about 13 to 15 minutes for the thighs and drumsticks. Drain the fried chicken on a paper towel-lined plate.

To make the Grilled Peaches: Slice the peaches in half. Place the halved peaches in a small bowl, drizzle with the olive oil and season with the salt and pepper. Preheat a grill or grill pan to medium-high heat. Grill the peaches for about 2 minutes on each side, so they have nice grill marks on both sides, but don't overcook them—you want a firm texture. Remove from the grill and set aside.

To serve, add a helping of fried chicken to each plate and top each with a Grilled Peach. Spoon over about ¼ cup of the Texas Peach-Whiskey Sauce and serve immediately.

BEVERAGE SUGGESTION

For this spicy fried chicken, a Whiskey Smash cocktail is the ideal match. Made with fresh mint, lemon juice, simple syrup, and good-quality Texas whiskey, the beverage offers bright citrus and herbal freshness that balances the heat and richness while the whiskey's warmth complements the peach-whiskey sauce.

Texas Cross Quail

with Sweet & Sour Orange Sauce

This bold and flavorful dish beautifully blends its smoky, tangy, and slightly sweet elements. The quail, marinated in warm spices and grilled to perfection, develops a crispy, charred exterior while remaining juicy inside. The sweet and sour orange sauce adds a bright, citrusy contrast with hints of honey, soy, and a touch of heat from red pepper flakes. This dish is a perfect fusion of Texas-style grilling and Asian-inspired flavors, making it an elegant yet rustic meal for a summer cookout.

Serves 4

Sweet & Sour Orange Sauce

Makes about 2 cups

1 cup fresh-squeezed orange juice
2 tablespoons honey
2 tablespoons rice or apple cider vinegar
1 tablespoon soy sauce
1 teaspoon peeled and grated fresh ginger
1 clove garlic, peeled and minced
½ teaspoon red pepper flakes
1 teaspoon cornstarch
1 tablespoon water
1 tablespoon unsalted butter

Grilled Texas Cross Quail

2 tablespoons extra-virgin olive oil
1 tablespoon freshly squeezed lemon juice
2 cloves garlic, peeled and minced

1 teaspoon ground smoked paprika
1 teaspoon ground cumin
1 teaspoon kosher salt
½ teaspoon fresh cracked black pepper
4 Texas Cross or other semi-boneless quail
Fresh cilantro leaves, for garnish
Chopped scallions, for garnish

To make the Sweet & Sour Orange Sauce: Add the orange juice, honey, vinegar, soy sauce, ginger, garlic, and red pepper flakes to a medium saucepan over medium heat. Bring to a simmer and cook for about 5 minutes. Whisk the cornstarch with the tablespoon of water in a small bowl to create a slurry. Stir in the cornstarch slurry and continue to simmer until the sauce thickens, about 2 more minutes. Remove from the heat and whisk in butter, allowing it to melt into the sauce. Reserve until ready for use. The sauce can be prepared up to 1 week ahead of time, reserved in an airtight container in the refrigerator. Gently rewarm before serving, stirring well.

To begin prepping the main dish, add the olive oil, lemon juice, garlic, smoked paprika, cumin, salt, and black pepper to a large bowl. Add the quail and rub the marinade all over the quail to coat. Marinate the quail for at least 30 minutes, or up to 4 hours, covered in the refrigerator.

Preheat a grill to medium-high heat, about 400°F. Add the quail to the grill breast-side down and grill for 3 to 5 minutes. Flip and continue cooking for another 3 to 5 minutes, until they are golden brown and cooked through; the internal temperature should reach 165°F. Remove from the grill and allow to rest for 5 minutes.

To serve, add grilled quail to a large platter and drizzle with warm Sweet & Sour Orange Sauce. Garnish with the cilantro and scallions and serve immediately.

BEVERAGE SUGGESTION

When it comes to Grilled Texas Cross Quail, reach for a vibrant Texas Tempranillo like the one from Becker Vineyards. The Tempranillo's bright red fruit and subtle spice complement the gamey richness of the bird and balance the citrusy sweetness.

PORK

If there's a protein that plays well across continents and comfort zones, it's pork—and it's one I turn to repeatedly for its sheer versatility. Whether I'm slow-roasting Yucatecan-style cochinita pibil until it falls apart into tender shreds or simmering silky pork cheeks into bacon-laced grits, I love how pork adapts to both bold spice and subtle finesse. Pozole verde is a longtime favorite in my kitchen, but I also lean into its more refined side—think prosciutto-wrapped loin over a Tuscan bean salad or a peach-glazed tenderloin brightened with citrus vinaigrette. What ties these dishes together for me is a deep sense of savor and satisfaction—built on long braises, spice-rubbed roasts, and vibrant, unexpected pairings. Pork proves its range in every bite: hearty yet nuanced, rustic yet refined.

Cherry-Braised Pork Cheeks

over Creamy Bacon Grits

Served over a bed of buttery, smoky bacon grits, this dish practically hugs you with comforting flavors. The grits get a little added salty depth from the bacon, while the pork cheeks are slowly braised in a flavorful mixture of vegetables, cherry purée, and beef consommé, resulting in a melt-in-your-mouth texture. The finishing cherry glaze adds a sweet and tangy contrast, complementing the richness of the pork. It's a soul-warming meal, perfect for a cold night spent cozied up on the couch. For the cherry purée, you can sometimes find it in grocery stores near the jams and jellies, or it is certainly available online. It's also a snap to make from frozen pitted cherries: Snag a 16-ounce bag. Allow the cherries to defrost at room temperature for 10 to 30 minutes. Toss the defrosted cherries into a high-powered blender or a food processor fitted with a blade attachment. Blend until smooth. Freeze into cubes or store in a jar in the fridge. This purée can stay in the fridge for 5 days, or in the freezer for up to 3 months.

Serves 6

Cherry-Braised Pork Cheeks

2 cups all-purpose flour
½ teaspoon kosher salt, more to taste
½ fresh cracked black pepper, more to taste
4 tablespoons extra-virgin olive oil, divided
5 pounds pork cheeks
2 carrots, peeled and diced
2 yellow onions, peeled and diced
2 celery stalks, diced
4 cloves garlic, peeled and minced

1 cup cherry purée
8 cups water
½ cup beef consommé or bouillon
Microgreens, for garnish, optional

Creamy Bacon Grits

Makes 8 cups

4 cups water or low sodium chicken broth
3 cups whole milk
1 tablespoon kosher salt
¼ teaspoon ground cayenne pepper
1 bacon slice, cooked and crumbled
1¼ cups stone-ground corn grits
3 to 5 tablespoons unsalted butter
¼ teaspoon fresh cracked black pepper, more to taste
3 large beaten eggs (optional)

To make the Pork: Preheat the oven to 350°F. Season the flour with salt and pepper in a shallow dish and lightly dredge the pork cheeks. Heat 2 tablespoons olive oil in a large sauté pan over medium-high. Sear the cheeks on both sides, working in batches if needed, then transfer to a roasting pan. Add the carrots, onions, and celery to the same pan and cook 3 to 4 minutes until softened. Stir in the garlic and cook 1 for minute. Add the cherry purée and reduce over medium heat for 5 minutes. Season as needed, then add the water and beef consommé. Bring to a boil and pour over the pork cheeks, making sure they are submerged. Cover with plastic wrap and foil, and braise 4 hours, until tender. Remove the cheeks and set aside.

Purée the vegetables and broth until smooth, strain, and return to the pot. Reduce by half at a simmer, about 10 minutes, and adjust seasoning. This glaze can be prepared ahead and refrigerated with the pork; rewarm gently before serving.

To make the Creamy Bacon Grits: Add the water or broth, milk, salt, cayenne, and bacon to a saucepan. Bring to a boil over medium-high, then whisk in the grits.

Reduce to medium and simmer, covered, about 30 minutes, stirring occasionally. Season with black pepper and adjust consistency with butter—start with 3 tablespoons and add up to 2 more for creaminess. For added richness, stir in beaten eggs. Serve immediately or refrigerate leftovers for 2 to 3 days.

To finish: Heat the remaining 2 tablespoons olive oil with the butter in a sauté pan. Sear the pork cheeks to warm through and form a crust. To assemble, spoon a serving of grits onto each plate, top with pork cheeks, drizzle with cherry glaze, and garnish with microgreens, if using. Serve hot.

BEVERAGE SUGGESTION

Pair these cherry-braised pork cheeks with a medium bodied Zinfandel, like Frank Family from Napa Valley. The Zin offers ripe dark fruit, subtle spice, and soft tannins that complement the rich, savory pork and smoky bacon while harmonizing with the sweet-tart cherry flavors.

Peach-Rubbed Pork Tenderloin

over Potato-Sausage Hash with Citrus Peach Vinaigrette

This dish places sweet, juicy, fragrant summer peaches right at center stage, using them two ways: in a garlicky, fruit-forward rub for the pork and in a bright citrus vinaigrette. The peach-rubbed pork tenderloin gets a golden sear before finishing in the oven, locking in flavor and juices, while a hearty hash of roasted potatoes, spicy sausage, and caramelized onions makes for a deeply satisfying base. A drizzle of the peachy vinaigrette brings it all into balance—sweet and savory at every bite. It's the kind of dish made to be shared around a long, sunny table on a beautiful summer's eve.

Citrus Peach Vinaigrette

Makes about 3 cups

1 peach, peeled, pitted, and chopped
1 shallot, peeled and chopped
½ cup rice wine vinegar
½ cup Sauvignon Blanc
½ cup extra-virgin olive oil
Zest from 2 lemons
Zest from 2 limes
Zest from 2 oranges, plus the chopped orange flesh from both

Peach-Rubbed Pork Tenderloin

1 peach, peeled, pitted, and chopped
1 Granny Smith apple, peeled, seeded, and chopped
1 segmented orange, peeled
5 cloves garlic, peeled
½ cup olive oil, plus 2 tablespoons, for searing
½ teaspoon kosher salt, more to taste

½ teaspoon fresh cracked black pepper, more to taste
2 (2-pound) whole pork tenderloins

Potato-Sausage Hash

Makes about 8 cups

4 to 6 cups (about 2 pounds) cubed Yukon Gold potatoes
2 tablespoons extra-virgin olive oil
¼ teaspoon kosher salt, more for finishing
¼ teaspoon fresh cracked black pepper, more for finishing
1 pound linguica or other spicy sausage
½ cup unsalted butter
2 peeled and chopped red onions
½ cup chopped fresh Italian flat-leaf parsley leaves

To make the Citrus Peach Vinaigrette: Add the peach, shallot, vinegar, and wine to a high-powered blender or food processor fitted with a blade attachment and blend until smooth. Transfer to a bowl, and then slowly whisk in the olive oil. Add the zest from the lemons, limes, and oranges, then toss in the chopped orange flesh. Set aside until ready for use. Any leftovers can be stored in the refrigerator for 2 to 3 days. Shake the vinaigrette well to reincorporate before using.

To make the Pork Tenderloin: Add the chopped peach, chopped apple, orange segments, garlic cloves, and the ½ cup of the olive oil to a high-powered blender or food processor fitted with a blade attachment. Blend the ingredients together until smooth. Add the salt and pepper, taste for seasoning, and add more, as desired. Note: You want the marinade to strike that nice salty-sweet balance; be sure you don't under salt. Place the pork tenderloins in a shallow dish and rub them all over with the peach marinade. Cover with plastic wrap and refrigerate the rubbed tenderloins for at least 2 hours, or up to overnight.

Preheat the oven to 400°F. Remove the pork tenderloins from the refrigerator, allowing them to sit out for a few minutes so that they aren't too cold when they hit the pan.

Heat the remaining 2 tablespoons olive oil in an oven-safe skillet over medium-high heat. Once the oil is shimmering, add the pork tenderloins and sear for about 2 to 3 minutes per side, until it develops a deep golden crust, about 6 to 8 minutes. Move the skillet with the seared pork directly into the preheated oven. Roast for 12 to 15 minutes, or until the internal temperature reaches 140–145°F for medium doneness.

Transfer the pork to a cutting board and let it rest for 5 to 10 minutes before slicing. This helps the juices redistribute and keeps it tender.

To prepare the Potato-Sausage Hash, preheat the oven to 400°F. Toss the cubed potatoes with olive oil, salt, and pepper on a large baking sheet and roast until golden and crispy, about 20 minutes. While they cook, brown the sausage in a sauté pan over medium-high heat, breaking it into bite-sized pieces, 5 to 6 minutes. Transfer to a plate. Return the pan to medium heat, melt the butter, and cook the onions until tender and caramelized. Add the roasted potatoes and sausage, tossing together for 2 to 3 minutes until combined. Remove from heat, stir in parsley, and adjust seasoning with salt and pepper. Keep warm.

To serve: Cut the tenderloins into medallions and place them over the Potato-Sausage Hash on a large serving platter. Drizzle with the Citrus Peach vinaigrette and serve immediately.

BEVERAGE SUGGESTION

Serve this pork tenderloin with a medium-bodied white wine like Viognier or an off-dry Riesling. These wines offer lush stone fruit flavors and balanced acidity that complement the sweetness of the peach rub and vinaigrette while cutting through the savory richness of the sausage and potatoes.

Prosciutto-Wrapped Pork Loin

over Tuscan Bean Salad with Blood Orange Vinaigrette

This dish brings together the sun-drenched flavors of the Italian countryside: salty, paper-thin slices of prosciutto envelop the tender pork loin, locking in moisture while adding a savory crispness as it sears and roasts. It's served over a warm Tuscan-style bean salad—creamy white beans tossed with sautéed peppers, briny kalamata olives, and fresh parsley—for a hearty, rustic base. A final drizzle of blood orange vinaigrette adds brightness and balance, echoing the citrus so often found in Italian coastal cooking.

Serves 6

Blood Orange Vinaigrette

Makes 2 cups

2 tablespoons Dijon mustard
1 cup fresh-squeezed blood orange juice
½ cup extra-virgin olive oil
⅛ teaspoon kosher salt, more to taste
⅛ teaspoon fresh cracked black pepper, more to taste

Tuscan Bean Salad

Makes about 8 cups

½ cup extra-virgin olive oil
½ cup diced red bell pepper
½ cup diced green bell pepper
½ cup peeled and diced red onion
½ cup chopped kalamata olives
¼ teaspoon kosher salt, more to taste

¼ teaspoon fresh cracked black pepper, more to taste
6 cups cooked or canned white beans, drained
¼ cup chopped fresh Italian flat-leaf parsley leaves

Prosciutto-Wrapped Pork Loin

6 (6-ounce) pork loin steaks
6 slices prosciutto
¼ teaspoon kosher salt
¼ teaspoon fresh cracked black pepper
2 tablespoons extra-virgin olive oil
Microgreens, for garnish, optional

To make the Blood Orange Vinaigrette: Add the Dijon mustard, blood orange juice, and olive oil to a small bowl and whisk well to combine. Season with salt and pepper, taste for seasoning, and add more, if desired. Set aside until ready to use. The vinaigrette can be prepared up to 3 days ahead of time and stored in an airtight container in the refrigerator. Shake or stir well to reincorporate before using.

To make the Tuscan Bean Salad: Heat the olive oil in a medium sauté pan over medium heat. Once shimmering, add the diced red and green peppers, red onions, and kalamata olives, sautéing them in olive oil until softened, about 3 to 4 minutes. Season with the salt and pepper. Toss the sautéed vegetables with the white beans and chopped parsley. Taste for seasoning, and add more salt and pepper, if desired. Serve warm.

To begin prepping the main dish, preheat the oven to 400°F.

Wrap each pork loin in a slice of prosciutto, then season with the salt and pepper. Heat the olive oil in an oven-safe skillet over medium-high heat. Sear the prosciutto-wrapped pork on all sides until golden.

Move the skillet with the seared pork directly into the preheated oven. Roast for 8 to 10 minutes, or until the internal temperature of the pork reaches 140–145°F for medium doneness. Remove from the oven and allow to rest for about 5 minutes.

To serve, spoon the Tuscan Bean Salad onto each plate. Slice the prosciutto-wrapped pork loins and place on top or around the beans. Drizzle the Blood Orange Vinaigrette over the pork and beans. Garnish with microgreens, if using, and serve.

BEVERAGE SUGGESTION

This pork loin recipe pairs nicely with a Chianti Classico or Sangiovese-based red wine. The wine's bright acidity and cherry fruit balance the saltiness of the prosciutto and cut through the richness of the pork while its earthy undertones complement the rustic beans and vibrant citrus vinaigrette.

Savory Pork Pozole Verde

with Tomatillo, Jalapeño & Pepita Seeds

Earthy, spicy, and deeply rooted in tradition, Pozole Verde de Puerco isn't just a soup—it's a celebration in a bowl. This vibrant green version of the classic Mexican dish gets its punch from fire-roasted tomatillos, jalapeños, and a generous handful of toasted pepita seeds, which give the broth its silky texture and subtle nuttiness. Fragrant with garlic, cilantro, and epazote, the broth cradles tender chunks of slow-simmered pork and toothsome hominy for a stew that's both comforting and electrifying. It's finished with an array of fresh garnishes—crisp cabbage, sharp radishes, and bright splashes of lime—that invite every diner to customize their bowl to their liking.

Serves 6

1 cup raw pepita (pumpkin) seeds
2 pounds boneless pork shoulder, diced
9 cups chicken stock or water
2½ teaspoons kosher salt, divided
½ teaspoon fresh cracked black pepper
1 dried bay leaf
1 pound husked tomatillos
1 large white onion, peeled and thinly sliced
6 cloves garlic, peeled and chopped
2 jalapeño peppers, quartered with seeds
¾ cup chopped fresh cilantro leaves, divided
1 teaspoon crumbled dried epazote or Mexican oregano
2 tablespoons vegetable oil
2 (15-ounce) cans white hominy, rinsed and drained

Diced radish, for serving
Shredded cabbage, for serving
Chopped white onion, for serving
Lime wedges, for serving
Dried oregano, for serving

Toast the pepita seeds in a small skillet over low heat, stirring occasionally until they puff up, about 6 to 7 minutes. Transfer to a bowl to cool.

Add the diced pork to a large stockpot or Dutch oven over medium heat, then add the chicken stock, 2 teaspoons of the salt, the pepper, and the bay leaf. Bring the mixture to a simmer and cook for 30 minutes, until the pork is cooked through. Strain off any fat from the surface, then separate out the pork from the stock in the pot, and reserve.

Add the tomatillos and sliced onions to the stock in the pot. Bring to a simmer and cook until the tomatillos and onions are tender, about 10 minutes. Add the toasted pepita seeds, as well as the garlic, the jalapeños with their seeds, ¼ cup of the cilantro, the epazote, and the other ½ teaspoon salt. Move the mixture to a high-powered blender or food processor fitted with a blade attachment, and blend well, working in batches, if needed.

Heat the vegetable oil in the same pot over medium-high heat. Once the oil is shimmering, add the puréed mixture back in and cook, uncovered, stirring frequently, until it thickens, about 10 minutes. Add the cooked pork and then the hominy to the pot and simmer, partially covered, for 20 minutes.

To finish, stir in the remaining ½ cup cilantro and serve the pozole warm in deep bowls with your choice of accompaniments: radish, cabbage, onion, lime wedges, and dried oregano.

BEVERAGE SUGGESTION

A tequila reposado from Casa Noble is a delicious addition to the savory pork pozole verde. The tequila's smooth, slightly aged character with hints of vanilla and caramel complement the earthy tomatillo and pepita seeds, while the subtle oak and warm spice balance the jalapeño's heat and the rich pork flavors.

Pozole

From Ancient Roots to Modern Tables

Pozole is more than just a stew—it's a cultural symbol, a dish rooted in tradition, history, and celebration. This hearty, soul-warming soup has been a part of Mexican cuisine for centuries, with its origins tracing back to ancient Aztec and Maya civilizations. The name "pozole" comes from the Nahuatl word pozolli, meaning "hominy," referring to the hulled corn kernels that form the base of the dish. There are three main types of pozole—white, red, and green—each with its own distinct preparation and regional variation. Pozole verde, like the version in this recipe, is known for its fresh, tangy flavors, with tomatillos and green chiles providing a bright contrast to the rich, savory broth. The beauty of pozole lies in its balance: the hominy provides chewiness and a comforting texture, while the tender pork infuses the broth with deep flavor. Toppings like radishes, lettuce, cilantro, and lime add freshness, and crunchy pepita seeds lend a delicious, nutty bite. Whether served during celebrations like Las Posadas or enjoyed on a cozy night in, pozole verde offers a perfect harmony of flavors that will transport you straight to the heart of Mexico.

Slow-Roasted Yucatecan Pork

with Sour Orange, Achiote & Red Onions

Savory, citrusy, and spicy, this dish, also known as cochinita pibil, is a celebration of Yucatán's culinary tradition. Marinated in a bright blend of vibrant achiote, sour orange juice, and garlic, the pork is slow cooked atop a bed of banana leaves, emerging tender and juicy from the oven. Set it out on a big platter along with warm corn tortillas, pickled red onions, and some spicy salsa, and you've got all the makings for an epic taco night. A couple notes on ingredients: Achiote paste is often found at Mexican food specialty stores, or it can be ordered online. If you have trouble finding fresh banana leaves at your grocery store, try the freezer aisle. To use in this recipe, simply defrost at room temperature before using them to line the roasting dish.

Serves 4

1 cup fresh sour orange juice
1 tablespoon apple or other cider vinegar
2 tablespoons achiote (annatto) paste
2 tablespoons peeled and chopped garlic
2 teaspoons kosher salt
3 pounds mixed boneless pork cuts, such as 2 diced shoulder steaks, plus 1 diced pork butt
8 to 10 banana leaves, more for serving
Warm corn tortillas, for serving

Pickled Red Onions

Makes 1½ cups

1 red onion, peeled and thinly sliced
1 cup water
1 cup apple cider vinegar

Charred Habanero Salsa

Makes approximately 1 cup

6 habanero chiles
1 yellow onion, peeled and quartered
½ cup fresh cilantro leaves
4 cloves garlic, peeled
2 tablespoons olive oil
Kosher salt and freshly cracked black pepper, to taste

Add the sour orange juice, cider vinegar, achiote (annatto) paste, garlic, and salt to a large bowl. Mix well to form a marinade. Add the pork to the bowl and rub the marinade thoroughly into the pork, ensuring all pieces are coated. Let the pork marinate at room temperature for 1 hour or refrigerate for at least 1 hour for deeper flavor.

Preheat the oven to 300°F.

Line a roasting pan with a layer of heavy-duty foil, followed by a layer of banana leaves. Arrange the marinated pork in the pan, making sure to pour the marinade over the meat. Cover the pan tightly with foil. Roast the pork for 3 to 4 hours, checking occasionally and turning the meat in its own juices. Cooking times may vary based on the toughness of the meat; you want the pork to be tender and almost falling-apart.

To make the Pickled Red Onions: Add the onion, water, and vinegar to a small saucepan over medium-high heat. Bring to a boil then turn off the heat. Let the onions cool completely in the liquid. Transfer to a covered container and refrigerate until ready to use. The onions will continue to develop flavor as they chill.

To make the Charred Habanero Salsa: Preheat the oven to 400°F. Add the chiles, onion, cilantro, and garlic to a roasting pan. Drizzle with olive oil and season lightly with salt and pepper, tossing to coat evenly. Roast until the vegetables are softened and deeply browned with light charring, 20 to 25 minutes, turning once if needed. Transfer the roasted ingredients to a mortar or blender and purée until smooth.

Add additional olive oil if necessary to reach the desired consistency. Taste and adjust seasoning before serving.

To serve, line a large serving platter with fresh banana leaves for presentation, then scatter the pork over top. Serve immediately with warm corn tortillas, also offering the Pickled Red Onions and Charred Habanero Salsa alongside.

BEVERAGE SUGGESTION

I enjoy a dark beer like a Mexican Negra Modelo with cochinita pibil. The beer's rich, roasted malt flavors and subtle sweetness complement the earthy achiote and caramelized pork while its smooth body balances the tangy citrus and spices for a harmonious, satisfying match.

VIBRANT ACHIOTE

Essential to Yucatecan Cooking

Achiote (also known as annatto) is a vibrant orange-red spice derived from the seeds of the Bixa orellana plant, native to the tropical Americas. Its earthy, slightly peppery flavor is a cornerstone of many Mexican and Central American dishes, particularly in the Yucatán region. When combined with sour orange juice, achiote becomes the perfect marinade for slow-roasted pork, infusing it with deep color and complexity. In Yucatecan cooking, recados (spice pastes) are often made with achiote as the base, blended with other ingredients like garlic, cumin, cloves, and oregano, forming the foundation for dishes like cochinita pibil. Achiote's flavor profile is subtle yet powerful, acting as a natural coloring agent for food while lending an earthy depth.

BEEF, LAMB & GAME

Beef, lamb, and game have always been some of my favorite proteins to cook with—they invite bold flavors, deep spices, and a slow-cooked tenderness that's hard to resist. Living in Texas, with its legendary love for beef, I've learned to appreciate how these meats can carry big, hearty flavors, like from cumin- and paprika-spiced beef empanadas served alongside bright chimichurri. But my inspiration doesn't stop there. I'm drawn to the globe-spanning stories these meats tell—from the warm spices of Lebanese lamb tartare and Friuli-style Italian lamb stew to the refined elegance of a Dijon-truffle-crusted rack of lamb. Whether it's pepper-crusted tenderloins with roasted chanterelles or wild boar chops glazed with a blackberry demi-glace, each dish is designed to impress, to satisfy, and to bring a modern edge to deeply rooted traditions.

Beer-Braised Beef Short Ribs

with Cheddar Cheese Grits & Spicy Fried Onion Rings

This rich and hearty dish delivers big on deep, comforting flavors. First, the short ribs are slow cooked in beer, allowing the meat to become incredibly tender and infused with rich, malty flavor. As they braise, the beef absorbs the savory broth, resulting in a succulent, melt-in-your-mouth texture. The dish is served over a creamy bed of cheddar cheese grits, which add a smooth, velvety texture with a sharp, cheesy bite. To finish, the crispy, golden fried onion rings are scattered over top to add a delightful crunch and a burst of heat, with the spicy zing cutting through the richness of the beef and grits. One tip: Take a cue from us at the restaurant and prep the short ribs a day in advance. An overnight hangout in the refrigerator really helps deepen the flavor. Plus, it makes your job much easier the next day—whip up the grits, fry some rings, and re-warm the ribs, and you are ready to eat.

Serves 6

Cheddar Cheese Grits

Makes 8 cups

4 cups water or low sodium chicken broth
3 cups whole milk
1 tablespoon kosher salt
¼ teaspoon ground cayenne pepper
1¼ cups stone-ground corn grits
1½ cups grated sharp cheddar cheese
3 to 5 tablespoons unsalted butter
⅛ teaspoon fresh cracked black pepper

Spicy Fried Onion Rings

Makes 10 to 12 onion rings

2 large yellow onions
¼ teaspoon kosher salt
¼ teaspoon fresh cracked black pepper
2 cups all-purpose flour
1 tablespoon ground cayenne pepper
1 tablespoon ground chili powder
6 cups vegetable or canola oil

Beer-Braised Short Ribs

2 cups all-purpose flour
1 teaspoon kosher salt, plus more for seasoning
1 teaspoon fresh cracked black pepper, plus more for seasoning
5 pounds whole bone-in beef short ribs
6 tablespoons vegetable or canola oil, divided
2 carrots, peeled and diced
2 yellow onions, peeled and diced
2 celery stalks, diced
4 cloves garlic, peeled
2 (12-ounce) bottles Shiner Bock or other dark beer
8 cups water
½ cup beef consommé or bouillon

To make the Cheddar Cheese Grits: Add the water or broth, milk, salt, and cayenne pepper to a medium saucepan over medium-high heat. Bring to a boil. Once boiling, slowly whisk in the grits, stirring to combine. Lower the heat to medium and bring to a simmer. Cover and cook, stirring occasionally, until thickened, about 30 minutes. Turn off the heat and stir in the cheese and 3 tablespoons of the butter until they both have melted into the grits, and the mixture is creamy, thick and smooth. If the mixture seems a little tacky or chunky, stir in the additional 2 tablespoons of butter. Season with pepper, adding more if desired, and serve immediately.

To make the Spicy Fried Onion Rings: Trim off the top and root ends of the onions and then slice them into ¼-inch-thick rings. Add the onions to a large mixing bowl and season with the salt and pepper, tossing the onions with your hands to coat with the seasonings. Add the flour, cayenne, and chili powder to another large mixing bowl, stirring to combine. Add the oil to a deep Dutch oven or frying pan over medium-high heat. Heat until the oil is shimmering. Transfer the onion rings to the bowl with the flour a few at a time, dredging the rings in the flour and coating each ring evenly in the mixture. Shake off any excess flour and then fry the onion rings in the hot oil in batches, until golden brown, about 3 to 4 minutes each. Remove with a slotted spoon and drain the onion rings on a paper towel-lined plated. Continue the frying process until all the onions are fried, allowing the oil to come back up to temperature in between. Serve the onion rings hot.

To begin the short ribs, preheat the oven to 350°F.

Add the flour to a large shallow dish and season with the salt and pepper. Gently pat the short ribs dry with a paper towel, then dredge the ribs in the flour, lightly coating all sides of the meat. Reserve on a plate.

Add 4 tablespoons of the oil to a large skillet over medium-high heat. Once the oil is shimmering, sear the short ribs in batches, about 5 minutes per side, flipping them over once or twice to create a nicely browned crust on the exterior. Remove the short ribs from the skillet and place in a large deep roasting pan. Chef's note: You'll want to use one that is big enough to hold all the ribs in a single layer, along with the vegetables and liquid. Place the diced carrots, onions, and celery, along with the garlic cloves, into the same pan on the stove and sauté for 2 to 3 minutes over medium-high heat until the veggies are tender. Add the beer and bring to a simmer. Allow to reduce at a simmer for about 5 minutes, stirring occasionally and scraping any browned bits off the sides and bottom of the pan. Check for seasoning at this point, and add more salt and pepper, if needed. Add the water and consommé or bouillon, bring to a boil, then pour over the ribs in the roasting pan, making sure they are completely submerged.

Cover first with plastic wrap and then with aluminum foil. Place the ribs in the oven and cook for 4 hours, or until very tender with the meat falling off the bones. When the ribs are cooked, remove from the oven and pull them out of the braising liquid with a pair of tongs, reserve the braising liquid for later. Let the ribs cool until you can handle them with your hands, about 10 to 15 minutes. Pick the meat off the bone, taking off as much fat as you can. Place the meat in a square plastic container or small cake pan and press down so that the meat is of a uniform thickness. Cover with plastic wrap and let cool completely in the refrigerator. Note: The ribs can be prepared to this point up to 1 day in advance.

To prep the sauce, take the reserved braising liquid and vegetables and add it to a high-powered blender or food processor fitted with a blade attachment. Purée on high speed until the vegetables are fully chopped and the broth is smooth. Strain the broth over a large pot using a fine mesh sieve to catch any large chunks left behind, then set the pot over medium-high heat. Bring the broth to a low boil. Simmer for about 10 minutes, until the broth has thickened and reduced by about half. Check for seasoning, adding more salt or pepper, if needed. Reserve until ready for use. Sauce can be prepped up to 1 day in advance as well. Reserve in a tightly covered container in the refrigerator and gently reheat on the stove before serving.

To serve: Pull the ribs from their container and cut into individual-sized square portions. Add the remaining 2 tablespoons oil to a large sauté pan and heat over medium-high. Once the oil is shimmering, sauté the short ribs in the hot oil, flipping them over a few times, until they are heated all the way through. Ladle the Cheddar Cheese Grits into the bottom of a very large serving tray or shallow bowl. Arrange the ribs over the grits, then drizzle over the sauce, and finally, top with the Spicy Fried Onions. Serve immediately.

BEVERAGE SUGGESTION

When enjoying beer-braised beef short ribs, I'll reach for a Shiner Bock. This smooth, malty Texas-style dark lager has just enough caramel sweetness and toasty depth to complement the richness of the short ribs and grits while its crisp finish balances the spice and crunch of the onion rings.

Beer + Beef

A Match Made in Heaven

Braising beef in beer is a time-honored technique that delivers deep flavor and irresistible tenderness. The beer not only helps break down tough cuts like short ribs but also infuses the meat with malty complexity. Dark beers—especially something like Shiner Bock, with its smooth, slightly sweet, roasted character—are especially good for this dish. The subtle bitterness balances the richness of the beef, while the malt enhances its caramelized flavors. Looking for a twist? Try a porter or stout for bolder, toastier notes, or a lighter ale if you want a brighter finish. Just steer clear of hoppy IPAs—their bitterness can overwhelm the dish.

Cumin- and Paprika-Spiced Beef Empanadas

with Green Olives, Raisins & Chimichurri Sauce

I'm including empanadas in my book as a personal tribute to my Argentine heritage. My grandfather was Argentinian, and growing up, empanadas were a staple in our home. Not only are they a beloved dish in Argentine cuisine, but they also hold a special place in my heart—the savory fillings wrapped in warm, golden dough remind me of family gatherings and the rich flavors of my grandfather's culture. My favorite version here features a fragrant, spiced beef filling that is brightened by the additions of raisins, chopped hard-boiled eggs, and briny green olives. Served with a punchy traditional chimichurri sauce, these empanadas embody tradition, love, and connection, making them the perfect addition to my story, and now yours as well.

Makes 12 empanadas

Chimichurri Sauce

Makes approximately 1 cup

1 teaspoon minced garlic
1/3 cup minced shallots
1 cup fresh Italian flat-leaf parsley leaves
1 teaspoon crushed red pepper flakes
2 tablespoons red wine vinegar
1/2 cup olive oil
1/8 teaspoon kosher salt, more to taste
1/8 teaspoon fresh cracked black pepper, more to taste

Cumin- and Paprika-Spiced Beef Empanadas

DOUGH

1 cup water

1 tablespoon kosher salt
1½ tablespoons lard or Crisco
3 cups all-purpose flour

FILLING

2 tablespoons olive oil
1 yellow onion, peeled and chopped
2 tablespoons chopped garlic
2 pounds 80/20 ground beef
2 tablespoons paprika
2 teaspoons cumin
1 teaspoon crushed red pepper flakes
½ cup raisins
1 cup pitted green olives, chopped
4 hard-boiled large eggs, peeled and whites and yolks chopped
⅛ teaspoon kosher salt, more to taste
⅛ teaspoon fresh cracked black pepper, more to taste
1 large egg, for brushing if baking
Neutral flavored oil, such as canola or vegetable, if frying

To make the Chimichurri Sauce: Add the garlic, shallots, parsley, and red pepper flakes to a food processor and combine. Add the vinegar, then drizzle in the oil as the machine is running until you end up with a chunky green sauce. Season with salt and pepper, taste for seasoning, and add more, if desired. The sauce can be prepped up to 1 week in advance; refrigerate in a tightly sealed container until ready to use. Any leftovers can be stored in the same manner, and it can also be frozen in chunks for later use.

To make the empanada dough: Over medium-high heat, add the water and salt in a large saucepan and bring to a boil. Then add the lard, mix well, and set aside to cool. Once cool, add the flour, 1 cup at a time, and work the dough with a spatula, until combined. The dough should be smooth, and elastic, with no excess flour left in the pan. Wrap the dough ball in plastic wrap and refrigerate for a minimum of 1 hour, or overnight for best results.

To make the filling: Add the olive oil to a medium sauté pan over medium heat. When oil is shimmering, add the onions and garlic and cook until translucent, about 3 to 5 minutes. Add the beef, paprika, cumin, and red pepper flakes, and cook until the meat is brown, about 8 to 10 minutes. Let cool and add the raisins, chopped olives, and eggs. Season with salt and pepper, taste for seasoning and add more, if desired. Allow to cool to room temperature. Note: The filling can be made up to 1 day ahead and refrigerated until ready to use.

To assemble: Roll out the chilled dough to a ¼-inch thickness. Using a cookie cutter, cut the dough into 4-inch diameter circles. Add about 2 tablespoons of stuffing to each dough, and close, crimping the edges with a fork to seal.

The empanadas can be fried or baked in the oven. To fry: Add the oil to a large frying pan until it is about 2 inches deep. You want to be able to fully submerge the empanadas in the oil as you fry. Bring the oil up to temperature over medium-high heat, until oil is shimmering. Carefully add a few empanadas at a time, allowing them plenty of space to cook, and fry in batches until golden brown, about 2 to 3 minutes each. Remove the empanadas with a slotted spoon and place on a paper towel-lined plate for several minutes to allow excess oil to drain before serving.

Chimichurri

Argentina's Culinary All-Star

In Argentina, chimichurri is traditionally served with grilled steak, or asado, but its uses extend far beyond that. It makes an incredible marinade or finishing sauce for any grilled or roasted meat, including lamb, chicken, and even fish. For these Cumin- and Paprika-Spiced Empanadas, chimichurri brings an added layer of freshness to the dish. The bright acidity from the vinegar and the herbaceous notes from the parsley and cilantro help balance the richness of the beef and the sweetness of the raisins. What makes chimichurri particularly special is its versatility. The core ingredients stay the same—herbs, oil, vinegar, and seasonings—but its flavor can be customized with a variety of add-ins like oregano, red pepper flakes, and onions. For an extra kick, you can add fresh chiles or a pinch of red pepper flakes to make it spicier. Chimichurri is one of those sauces that evolves as it sits, developing new layers of flavor the longer it's allowed to rest, so I always let mine hang out in the refrigerator for at least a day or two before using.

To bake: Preheat the oven to 350°F. Arrange the empanadas on a baking sheet, brush each lightly with egg wash, and poke the top of each lightly with a fork to allow for venting. (Note: To create the wash, crack an egg into a small bowl, add 1 tablespoon of water, then whisk together to combine.) Bake the empanadas for about 20 minutes, or until golden brown. Remove from the oven and allow to cool for several minutes before serving. For either preparation, serve the empanadas warm with a side of Chimichurri Sauce.

BEVERAGE SUGGESTION

These beef empanadas pair beautifully with a classic Argentine Malbec. Its deep plum and blackberry notes, soft tannins, and hints of spice complement the savory-sweet filling while its bold character stands up to the richness of the pastry and the herbaceous brightness of the chimichurri.

Grilled Beef Tenderloins over New Potatoes

with Roasted Chanterelles & Béarnaise Sauce

This rich and indulgent dish allows the natural flavors of the beef to shine. The tenderloin is seasoned simply with salt and pepper, then grilled, offering a nice sear on the outside while remaining tender and juicy on the inside. The golden and delicate chanterelle mushrooms are roasted to bring out their earthy, slightly fruity flavor. They add a soft, buttery texture that complements the richness of the beef. The béarnaise sauce, a creamy and tangy French sauce made from egg yolks, butter, tarragon, and shallots, brings a velvety smooth texture and a slight herbal note that balances the richness of the meat and mushrooms. Added on top of Roasted New Potatoes and the finished dish really sings.

Serves 6

Roasted New Potatoes

Makes about 8 cups

2 pounds new potatoes
2 teaspoons extra-virgin olive oil
Fresh cracked black pepper, to taste
Kosher salt, to taste

Roasted Chanterelles

Makes 4 cups

4 to 6 cups chanterelle mushrooms
¼ cup olive oil
⅛ teaspoon kosher salt
⅛ teaspoon fresh cracked black pepper
½ teaspoon chopped fresh thyme leaves

Béarnaise Sauce

Makes 1½ cups

¼ cup white wine vinegar
¼ cup dry white wine
1 tablespoon peeled and minced shallots
1 tablespoon dried tarragon
3 large egg yolks
1 cup melted unsalted butter
2 tablespoons minced fresh tarragon
⅛ teaspoons kosher salt
⅛ teaspoon fresh cracked black pepper

Grilled Beef Tenderloins

6 (10-ounce) beef tenderloin fillets
3 tablespoons cracked black pepper
1 tablespoon kosher salt
2 tablespoons extra-virgin olive oil

To make the Roasted New Potatoes: Preheat the oven to 350°F. Wash the potatoes, pat dry, and cut into quarters. Toss with olive oil, salt, and pepper, then arrange on a sheet pan in a single layer. Roast until golden brown and slightly crispy, about 15 minutes. Keep warm until ready to serve.

To make the Roasted Chanterelles: Preheat the oven to 400°F. Wash the mushrooms in a colander and let air dry for 5 to 10 minutes. Pat away any excess moisture, then slice into halves or quarters if large. Add to a bowl and toss with olive oil, salt, pepper, and fresh thyme. Spread on a baking sheet and roast for 10 to 12 minutes, or until soft and browned. Reserve until ready for use.

To make the Béarnaise Sauce: Add the vinegar, wine, shallots, and dried tarragon to a small saucepan. Simmer over medium heat for 5 to 10 minutes until reduced to about 2 tablespoons. Remove from the heat, cool to room temperature, and strain through a fine sieve. Place egg yolks in a high-powered blender or food processor and blend. With the blade running, slowly pour in the melted butter until incorporated and the sauce is fluffy. Stir in the reduction and fresh tarragon, then season with salt and pepper. Reserve until ready for use. The sauce can be prepared a few hours ahead and refrigerated in an airtight container. Rewarm gently in a saucepan before serving. Leftovers will keep for 2 to 3 days.

To prepare the beef: Remove the tenderloins from the refrigerator and let sit at room temperature for 30 minutes. Preheat a grill or grill pan to medium-high heat. Mix salt and pepper on a baking sheet. Pat the tenderloins dry, roll in the seasoning, and rub with olive oil. Place the fillets on the grill and sear on both sides until grill marks appear and a brown crust forms. Lower the heat to medium, cover, and cook over indirect heat until the internal temperature reaches 125°F for rare, 130°F for medium-rare, or 140°F for medium. This will take 15 to 25 minutes, with one turn of the meat during cooking. Transfer to a cutting board and rest for 10 to 15 minutes before slicing.

To serve: Place Roasted New Potatoes on each plate, top with a tenderloin, add Roasted Chanterelles, and finish with a generous spoonful of Béarnaise Sauce. Serve immediately.

BEVERAGE SUGGESTION

Grilled beef tenderloin over roasted new potatoes is an exquisite match with a big Napa Cabernet Sauvignon like a Darioush Caravan. The wine's bold tannins, rich dark fruit, and hints of oak stand up to the decadence of the Béarnaise and the umami of the chanterelles while its structure and depth perfectly complement the tender, grilled beef.

Dijon- and Truffle-Crusted Rack of Lamb

with Savory Wild Mushroom Bread Pudding & Lamb Jus

This elegant entrée is the heart and soul of Salum, proudly standing as our most popular dish for the past twenty years. A timeless favorite, it has consistently captured the taste buds of our guests with its perfectly seasoned, tender meat and beautifully caramelized crust. This iconic dish has remained a cornerstone of our menu, embodying the essence of quality and tradition that we are known for. Complemented by a mushroom bread pudding, this rack of lamb is an unforgettable plate that keeps our guests coming back time and time again, and we bet it will have your guests at home feeling the same way. If you are lucky enough to have access to fresh truffles, shave a few thin slices into the crust mixture here. If not, canned truffle peelings are wonderful and readily available to order online.

Serves 4

Wild Mushroom Bread Pudding

Serves 6 to 8

1 baguette loaf
2 tablespoons unsalted butter
4 cups washed and cleaned wild mushrooms
4 large beaten eggs
2 cups heavy cream
1 cup grated Parmesan cheese
¼ teaspoon kosher salt
¼ teaspoon fresh cracked black pepper

Dijon- and Truffle-Crusted Rack of Lamb

1 full 8-rib rack of lamb

½ teaspoon kosher salt
½ teaspoon fresh cracked black pepper
¼ cup Dijon mustard
½ cup panko Japanese breadcrumbs
2 to 3 thinly sliced truffle peels
¼ teaspoon truffle oil
1 cup lamb demi-glace

To make the Wild Mushroom Bread Pudding: Slice the baguette into ½-inch cubes and place in a large bowl. Allow the bread to sit out for at least 30 minutes, or up to several hours to help it dry out. Melt the butter in a medium-sized pan over medium heat. Add the mushrooms and sauté until tender, about 5 to 7 minutes. Remove from the heat and set aside. Preheat the oven to 350°F. Add the mushrooms to the bread in the bowl. Add the beaten eggs, heavy cream, Parmesan cheese, salt and pepper, and stir with a non-stick spatula or spoon until well combined. Pour the bread pudding into a greased baking dish and bake in the oven for 20 minutes, or until the top has a nice, caramelized color and the pudding is set. Serve warm, sliced in wedges.

Pat the rack of lamb dry with a paper towel. Season generously with the salt and pepper. Set a large sauté pan over medium-high heat. Once the pan is hot, sear the lamb on one side, about 5 to 6 minutes, until a nice brown crust forms. Remove from the heat.

Preheat the oven to 450°F.

Cover the entire rack with an even layer of the Dijon mustard using a pastry brush. Add the panko breadcrumbs, truffle peels, and truffle oil to a small bowl, and stir together. Using your hands, encrust the entire rack with the panko mixture, pushing it gently into the Dijon to adhere.

Place the encrusted lamb in a large roasting pan, with the seared side facing up. Roast in the oven until the lamb reaches your desired doneness: 15 to 20 minutes for medium-rare, or until the temperature reaches 130-135°F; or roast for an additional 3 to 5 minutes for medium, or until the temperature reaches 135-145°F.

Remove the lamb from the oven and allow to rest for 5 to 10 minutes to help redistribute the meat juices. While the lamb is resting, deglaze the roasting pan with the lamb demi-glace, stirring the demi-glace into any of the juices left in the pan with a wooden spoon until smooth.

To serve, cut the lamb into double chop portions. On each plate, place a lamb chop and spoon over a few tablespoons of the demi-glace sauce. Serve with a wedge or slice of the Wild Mushroom Bread Pudding alongside.

BEVERAGE SUGGESTION

This signature lamb dish is elevated when enjoyed with a Bordeaux blend (especially from the Left Bank, like Pauillac or Margaux) or Napa Valley Cabernet Sauvignon. These structured, full-bodied reds offer deep cassis, earth, and herb notes that complement the lamb's richness, echo the umami of the mushrooms, and stand up to the decadence of the truffle and jus with elegance and power.

Friuli-Style Italian Lamb Stew

with Red Wine, Garlic & Cinnamon

Spezzatino di Agnello alla Friulana is a traditional Italian dish from the Friuli-Venezia Giulia region, located in the northeastern part of Italy. Known for its rich and hearty flavor, the stew typically includes tender pieces of lamb, which are browned in olive oil and then slowly simmered with a combination of vegetables such as onions, carrots, celery, and garlic. The key to its depth of flavor lies in the use of red wine, which is added to deglaze the pan and help tenderize the meat. The lamb is then cooked for hours until tender and the flavors have melded together. The addition of cinnamon gives it a unique twist compared to other lamb stews, and it often has a slightly tangy undertone from the wine.

Serves 4

1 ⅓ pounds boneless lamb leg or shoulder
5 tablespoons extra-virgin olive oil
2 slices bacon, chopped
1 yellow onion, peeled and minced
2 cloves garlic, peeled and minced
¼ teaspoon kosher salt, more as needed
¼ teaspoon fresh cracked black pepper, more as needed
1 tablespoon all-purpose flour
8 cups beef broth or stock
1 cup dry red wine
2 tablespoons tomato paste
½ teaspoon ground cinnamon

Cut the lamb into 1-inch cubes and set aside. Heat the olive oil in a large, heavy-bottom Dutch oven or pot over medium heat until shimmering. Add the chopped bacon,

onion, and garlic, and cook until the bacon is rendered and crisp, and the garlic and onions are tender and fragrant, about 5 to 6 minutes.

Gradually add the lamb cubes in batches, and brown the lamb evenly on all sides, creating a nice crust on all the pieces. Season with the salt and pepper and then dust with the flour. Cook for 2 to 3 minutes, allowing the flour mixture to brown slightly. Add in the beef stock, stir, and bring the stew to a simmer. Cook for 30 minutes, stirring occasionally to avoid any lamb or veggies sticking to the bottom of the pot.

After 30 minutes of cooking, add the red wine and season with cinnamon. Taste for seasoning and add more salt and pepper, as needed. Stir in the tomato paste, stirring well to combine. Bring the stew back up to a low simmer and cook an additional 30 minutes to 1 hour, until the lamb is fork-tender, and the sauce is very thick. Serve in bowls, ladled over soft polenta or mashed potatoes, and with a side of crusty bread.

BEVERAGE SUGGESTION

Enjoy a Refosco dal Peduncolo Rosso, a native red wine from Friuli, with this Friuli-style Italian lamb stew. The wine's deep plum and black cherry notes, firm tannins, and subtle herbal-spice profile complement the richness of the lamb and echo the warm spice of the cinnamon, creating a beautifully regional and harmonious pairing.

Lebanese Lamb Tartare

with Nutty Bulgur & Fragrant Warming Spices

Elegant and earthy, Kibbeh Nayyeh is a classic Lebanese preparation of finely ground raw lamb, bulgur, and warm spices like allspice, cinnamon, and cumin. Traditionally served as part of a mezze spread, it's a dish that highlights the beauty of simplicity and freshness—made with care, served immediately, and best enjoyed with plenty of good olive oil, herbs, and warm pita for scooping. This version stays true to tradition while emphasizing quality ingredients and textural balance.

Serves 4

1 cup fine bulgur wheat
1 pound finely ground fresh lamb
1 small white onion, peeled and finely grated
1 teaspoon ground allspice
½ teaspoon ground cinnamon
½ teaspoon ground cumin
½ teaspoon kosher salt
¼ teaspoon fresh cracked black pepper
1 tablespoon olive oil, plus additional as needed
¼ cup chopped fresh mint leaves
¼ cup toasted pistachios or pine nuts
Lemon wedges, for serving

Add the bulgur to a medium mixing bowl. Pour over enough cold water to completely immerse the bulgur, then soak in the cold water for about 30 minutes, or until the bulgur is tender, but still has some bite to it. Drain the water from the bulgur using a fine mesh sleeve or small colander, pressing down gently with the back of your hand to ensure you squeeze out any excess water. Set aside.

WHERE MEMORY MEETS MEZZE

A Taste of My Grandmother's Kitchen

Kibbeh Nayyeh holds a particularly special place in my heart, evoking memories of my Lebanese grandmother's kitchen. This traditional dish was a labor of love that brought our family together around the table. Now I've perfected my own version, and each bite is a taste of tradition, a link to my roots, and a reminder of the warmth and care my grandmother poured into every meal. A few tips to success with this dish: Freshness is key, so find high-quality meat from a trusted butcher, if possible, especially if you are concerned about eating raw meat. We always ask our butcher to grind the lamb twice to ensure a beautifully smooth texture, and the Kibbeh Nayyeh is at its best immediately after preparation.

Add the ground meat, soaked and drained bulgur, grated onion, allspice, cinnamon, cumin, salt, and black pepper to the bowl of a food processor fitted with a blade attachment. Pulse for several minutes until the mixture is well-combined and smooth. Chef's note: You can also mix by hand in a large bowl, kneading the mixture together with your hands. If the mixture is a little dry, you can add in about 1 tablespoon olive oil.

Shape the lamb tartare into a smooth flat round or oval, depending on the size and shape of the serving dish you would like to use. You can also shape it into small mounds or individual patties if you prefer.

To serve, place the tartare on your serving tray and drizzle with a few teaspoons of olive oil. Sprinkle the chopped fresh mint leaves and nuts on top for added flavor and texture. Serve with fresh lemon wedges on the side for squeezing over the kibbeh.

BEVERAGE SUGGESTION

When sitting down with this Lebanese preparation, I will reach for a dry Rosé from Lebanon (like Château Musar Jeune Rosé). The wine's bright acidity, subtle red fruit, and floral notes lift the richness of the meat while complementing the herbs and spices without overpowering them. Another option is Arak, Lebanon's iconic anise-flavored spirit—a classic and culturally rooted match. When diluted with water, the Arak's cool licorice notes cleanse the palate and contrast beautifully with the richness of the meat and the spice of the dish.

Rosemary-Thyme Wild Boar Chops

with Blackberry Demi-Glace

This rich and flavorful dish elevates the robust, slightly gamey taste of wild boar with a luxurious, fruity sauce. The wild boar chops are seasoned with aromatic rosemary and thyme, then seared before being roasted to a tender finish. The accompanying blackberry demi-glace adds depth and complexity, made with fresh blackberries, red wine, and wild game stock, balanced with a touch of balsamic vinegar and honey for a harmonious sweet-tart contrast. The result is a beautifully sophisticated dish.

Serves 4

Blackberry Demi-Glace

Makes 2 cups

1 tablespoon butter
1 peeled and finely chopped shallot
1 cup fresh or frozen blackberries, plus more for garnish
½ cup Cabernet Sauvignon, or other robust red wine
½ cup wild game or beef stock
¼ cup balsamic vinegar
1 tablespoon honey
¼ teaspoon kosher salt, more to taste
¼ teaspoon fresh cracked black pepper, more to taste

Rosemary-Thyme Wild Boar Chops

8 bone-in wild boar chops
1 tablespoon finely chopped fresh rosemary leaves, plus more for garnish
1 tablespoon finely chopped fresh thyme leaves, plus more for garnish
½ teaspoon kosher salt, more to taste

½ teaspoon fresh cracked black pepper, more to taste
2 tablespoons extra-virgin olive oil
2 cloves garlic, peeled and minced
1 tablespoon butter

To make the Blackberry Demi-Glace: Melt the butter in a medium saucepan over medium heat. Add the shallots and cook until softened, about 2 to 3 minutes. Add the blackberries, red wine, wild game or beef stock, balsamic vinegar, and honey to the pan. Season with the salt and pepper. Stir to combine. Bring the mixture to a simmer and cook for 10 to 15 minutes, occasionally stirring, until the sauce reduces and thickens slightly. Strain the sauce through a fine-mesh sieve layered over a bowl to remove any solids and return the liquid to the saucepan. Let it simmer over medium heat for an additional 5 minutes, adjusting seasoning with salt and pepper to taste. Once it reaches a demi-glace consistency—thick, but still pourable—remove from the heat. Set aside at room temperature until ready to use. Any leftovers can be stored in the refrigerator in an airtight container for up to 1 week.

Preheat the oven to 375°F.

Allow the wild boar chops to come to room temperature, then season the wild boar chops with the rosemary, thyme, salt and pepper. Set aside.

Heat the olive oil in a large, oven-safe skillet over medium-high heat. Add the garlic and cook for about 1 minute, until fragrant. Place the boar chops in the skillet and sear them for 3 to 4 minutes on each side, until browned. Note: You can do this in batches, if needed. Once all the chops have been seared, place them in the oven, in the cooking skillet, and roast for 8 to 10 minutes. Depending on the thickness, this timing should give you a nice, medium chop at 140-145°F. If you prefer a medium to medium-well cook, roast for an additional 3 to 5 minutes, or until the internal temperature on the chops reaches 150-155°F.

Remove the chops from the oven, add a pat of butter on top of each chop, and let them rest for 5 minutes. To serve, place the wild boar chops on a serving platter and drizzle the Blackberry Demi-glace over the top. Garnish with fresh herbs or extra blackberries, as desired.

BEVERAGE SUGGESTION

These wild boar chops find their perfect pairing with a Petite Sirah from Napa Valley. The bold reds offer dark berry fruit, earthy undertones, and firm tannins that echo the rich, gamey flavor of the boar and complement the sweet-tart depth of the blackberry sauce while the herbal notes in the wine harmonize with the rosemary and thyme.

Elevate Your Game

Cooking with Wild Boar

Wild boar offers a bold, slightly gamey alternative to pork, with a deeper, richer flavor and leaner texture. Though it's in the pig family, wild boar has a darker, redder meat that stands up beautifully to strong herbs like rosemary and thyme and benefits from being paired with fruit-based sauces like this blackberry demi-glace. Boar is naturally lower in fat than domestic pork, so it's best cooked to medium rare or medium to avoid drying out, with a good sear to lock in juices. Look for responsibly sourced wild boar from specialty butchers or online purveyors—it's becoming more available thanks to growing interest in game meats. If you're new to boar, think of it as pork's rugged cousin—earthier, leaner, and made for bold, savory dishes.

FISH & SHELLFISH

Often called the "fruits of the sea," fresh seafood is already a treasure—but in my kitchen, these gifts get a bold, unexpected lift. I love layering vibrant spices, bright sauces, and inventive sides to bring each dish alive, whether it's pan-seared halibut with a fragrant za'atar crust resting on crispy chickpea croquettes or Yucatecan-style redfish wrapped in banana leaves and accented by a bright achiote sauce. Every plate is about balancing depth and brightness to celebrate what the ocean offers—which is just the way I like it.

PAN-SEARED HALIBUT WITH ZA'ATAR CRUST

over Chickpea Croquettes & Saffron Tomato Sauce

More than just a meal, this dish is an experience—one that fills the kitchen with the scents I most associate with my grandmother's cooking: za'atar, saffron, tomatoes, chickpeas. Plated, the dish is a beautiful contrast of textures and colors—the deep red sauce cradling the golden chickpea croquettes, the perfectly seared, za'atar-encrusted halibut resting on top, and a scattering of fresh herbs adding a final touch of brightness. The first bite is both familiar and new, a taste of the past woven into something fresh and elegant.

Serves 6

Za'atar Crust

Makes about 1/4 cup

6 teaspoons dried thyme
2 teaspoons powdered sumac
2 teaspoons toasted sesame seeds
1/2 teaspoon kosher salt

Chickpea Croquettes

Makes about 12 croquettes

1 pound dried chickpeas
1 small white onion, peeled and coarsely chopped
2 cloves garlic, peeled and crushed
1 tablespoon all-purpose flour
1 teaspoon ground coriander

1 teaspoon baking soda
½ teaspoon ground cumin
¼ teaspoon kosher salt, more to taste
¼ teaspoon fresh cracked black pepper, more to taste
½ cup vegetable oil, for frying

Saffron Tomato Sauce

Makes about 4 cups

2 tablespoons extra-virgin olive oil
1 yellow onion, peeled and chopped
¼ cup peeled and chopped garlic
4 tomatoes, peeled and seeded
¼ teaspoon saffron threads
¼ teaspoon kosher salt, more to taste
¼ teaspoon fresh cracked black pepper, more to taste

Pan-Seared Halibut

6 (7-ounce) skin-off halibut fillets
½ teaspoon kosher salt
½ teaspoon fresh cracked black pepper
4 tablespoons extra-virgin olive oil
Microgreens or chopped Italian flat-leaf parsley leaves, for garnish

To make the Za'atar Crust: Add the thyme, sumac, sesame seeds, and salt to a spice grinder. Pulse until a fine powder forms, about 30 seconds. Store in an airtight container at room temperature for up to 2 months.

To prepare the Chickpea Croquettes: Place the chickpeas in a mixing bowl and cover with cold water. Cover and soak overnight in the refrigerator. Drain and pat dry. Transfer to a food processor with the onion, garlic, flour, coriander, baking soda, cumin, salt, and pepper. Process until smooth, adjusting seasoning as needed. Shape into small patties, about ½ cup each. Heat vegetable oil in a heavy-bottomed pan over medium-high heat. Fry the patties in batches until golden brown. Drain on paper towels and keep warm.

To make the Saffron Tomato Sauce: Heat the olive oil in a saucepan over medium heat. Add the onions and garlic, cover, and cook for 4 to 5 minutes. Stir in the tomatoes and saffron, then cook for 15 minutes. Transfer to a blender and pulse, leaving some texture. Season with salt and pepper. The sauce can be made up to 1 week ahead and refrigerated in an airtight container. Rewarm before serving.

To prepare the fish: Preheat the oven to 375°F. Let the halibut sit at room temperature for 5 to 10 minutes. Season with salt and pepper. Heat the olive oil in an oven-safe sauté pan over high heat. Sear on one side until golden brown, then flip and sprinkle 1 teaspoon of the Za'atar Crust over each portion. Transfer to the oven and roast for 5 to 8 minutes, or until cooked through.

To assemble: Spoon about ½ cup of Saffron Tomato Sauce onto each plate. Place 1 or 2 Chickpea Croquettes in the center, top with halibut, and garnish with microgreens or parsley. Serve hot.

BEVERAGE SUGGESTION

Pan-seared halibut united with a crisp, aromatic Assyrtiko from Greece or a dry Rosé from the Mediterranean is simply delicious. Assyrtiko's bright acidity and mineral notes highlight the citrusy, herbal za'atar and cut through the richness, while a dry rosé adds refreshing red fruit and subtle earthiness that complement the saffron and chickpeas.

Pan-Seared Sea Bass

with Pumpkin Bisque, Brussels Sprout–Chorizo Sauté, and Dukkah Dust

This dish is one of those "wow" plates: the sea bass gets a beautiful, golden sear that locks in its flaky tenderness, and it sits on a pool of creamy pumpkin bisque that brings just the right amount of cozy warmth. The Brussels sprouts and chorizo add a smoky-sweet crunch that keeps things interesting, and the dukkah dusting? That's the secret weapon—nutty, aromatic, and just enough texture to make every bite pop. It's a dish that's just as fun to plate as it is to eat.

Serves 6

Dukkah Dust

Makes about ½ cup

2 tablespoons hazelnuts
1½ tablespoons sesame seeds
1 teaspoon coriander seeds
1 teaspoon cumin seeds
1 teaspoon fennel seeds
1 teaspoon whole black peppercorns
¼ teaspoon kosher salt

Brussels Sprout–Chorizo Sauté

Makes about 2 cups

1 tablespoon extra-virgin olive oil
½ cup peeled and finely diced yellow onion
1 clove garlic, peeled and minced
¼ cup sliced Spanish chorizo
1½ cups cored and thinly sliced Brussels sprouts

1/8 teaspoon kosher salt, more to taste
1/8 teaspoon fresh cracked black pepper, more to taste
2 tablespoons white balsamic vinegar
1 tablespoon unsalted butter

Pumpkin Bisque

Makes 8 cups

1 tablespoon extra-virgin olive oil
3/4 cup peeled and sliced yellow onions
2 garlic cloves, peeled and minced
2 cups peeled, roasted and puréed pumpkin, or 1 (15-ounce) can pumpkin purée
6 cups chicken stock or water
1/4 teaspoon ground cayenne pepper
1/4 teaspoon ground nutmeg
3/4 cup heavy cream
1/4 teaspoon kosher salt, more to taste
1/4 teaspoon fresh cracked black pepper, more to taste

Pan-Seared Sea Bass

6 (5- to 6-ounce) skin-off sea bass fillets
1/2 teaspoon kosher salt, more for finishing
1/2 teaspoon fresh cracked black pepper
2 tablespoons extra-virgin olive oil

To make the Dukkah Dust: Preheat the oven to 350°F. Spread the hazelnuts in a single layer on a baking sheet. Roast for about 10 to 15 minutes, shaking the pan once or twice, until the skins darken and the nuts are golden and fragrant. Note: Keep an eye on them—they can go from toasted to burnt quickly. Transfer the hot hazelnuts to a clean kitchen towel. Rub them together vigorously in the towel to remove the skins. Don't worry if some skins stay on; it's fine if they're not completely bare. Cool completely. While the hazelnuts cool, toast the sesame, coriander, cumin and fennel seeds alongside with the peppercorns in a hot pan over medium heat until aromatic, about 2 to 3 minutes. Let cool, then add the hazelnuts along with the spice mixture to a food processor fitted with a blade attachment. Add the salt and pulse all ingredients into a fine dust. The Dukkah Dust can be prepared up to 1 week in advance. Store in an airtight container in a cool, dry place; any extra seasoning will keep for up to 1 month.

To prepare the Brussels Sprout–Chorizo Sauté: Heat the oil in a medium skillet or sauté pan over medium heat until shimmering. Add the onions and garlic and sauté until softened, about 2 to 3 minutes. Add the chorizo and cook for a few minutes to release flavors. Stir in Brussels sprouts, season with the salt and pepper, and then deglaze with the vinegar, tossing the ingredients to coat. Taste for seasoning and add more salt and pepper, if desired. Finish with the butter, removing the vegetables from the heat as soon as it is melted to ensure the Brussels sprouts remain crisp. Serve immediately.

To make the Pumpkin Bisque: Add the oil to a large stock pot or Dutch oven and heat over medium heat until shimmering. Add the onions and garlic and sauté until fragrant, about 2 to 3 minutes. Add the pumpkin purée, stock or water, cayenne, and nutmeg. Bring to a simmer. Stir in the heavy cream and then season with the salt and pepper. Taste for seasoning, and add more salt and pepper, if desired. Purée the soup with an immersion blender, or transfer to a food processor fitted with a blade attachment, and blend until smooth and light. Turn the heat to low and leave on the stove while preparing the sea bass. The bisque can be prepped up to 2 to 3 days ahead of time, stored in an airtight container in the refrigerator. Rewarm before using.

Season the sea bass with the salt and pepper and allow it to sit out at room temperature for a few minutes so it isn't too cold when it hits the pan.

Preheat the oven to 400°F. Heat the olive oil in a large, oven-safe sauté pan and then sear the sea bass fillets, until golden brown. Transfer the sea bass to the oven and roast until the fish is cooked through, anywhere from 10 to 18 minutes depending

The Perfect Finishing Touch

A Sprinkle of Dukkah Dust

Dukkah, a popular Egyptian spice blend, has been captivating palates for centuries with its unique combination of nuts, seeds, and spices. This dust instantly tantalizes with its earthy richness and aromatic crunch. Hazelnuts form the base of the mix, adding a toasty, slightly sweet flavor, while sesame seeds provide nuttiness and a delicate bite. Coriander, cumin, fennel, and black peppercorns contribute complexity with citrusy, warm, and savory notes. When prepared in advance, it's an easy pantry staple that you can sprinkle over soups, salads, or any savory dish that needs an extra kick. The nuts and seeds lend satisfying crunch, and the spices bring a burst of depth that works beautifully in Mediterranean and Middle Eastern-inspired meals.

on the thickness of your fillets. Note: A good rule of thumb is to cook fish for 10 minutes per inch of thickness. The fish is done when it's opaque throughout and flakes easily with a fork.

To plate the dish, pour about ½ cup of Pumpkin Bisque into the base of a soup bowl. Place a generous spoonful of Brussels Sprout-Chorizo Sauté in the center and top with the seared sea bass fillet. Finish with a sprinkle of Dukkah Dust over the fish. Serve immediately.

Beverage Suggestion

There's nothing like pan-seared sea bass and a Lebanese white wine like Château Musar White or a crisp white from the Eastern Mediterranean. These wines offer bright acidity, subtle minerality, and herbal notes that bring out the rich pumpkin bisque, savory chorizo, and nutty, aromatic flavors of the Dukkah, creating a balanced and vibrant Middle Eastern-inspired pairing.

Yucatecan-Style Redfish Wrapped in Banana Leaves

with Citrusy Achiote Sauce

Tikin Xic is a traditional Yucatecan dish known for its vibrant flavors and distinctive cooking method. It typically features fish, most often red snapper, that is marinated in a blend of orange juice, garlic, and achiote, a spice and vibrant coloring agent extracted from the seeds of an achiote tree that grows in the tropics. It is commonly found in Mexican dishes and Caribbean cuisine, where it is sometimes also referred to as annatto. Here, the marinated fish is wrapped in banana leaves, which helps to retain moisture and infuse the fish with a subtle earthy flavor, and baked, resulting in a dish that's tender, aromatic, and bursting with citrusy, savory, and slightly smoky notes from the achiote. It's also a real showpiece of a dish, as the bright red sauce is revealed as you unwrap the tender, flaky fish.

Serves 6

Citrusy Achiote Sauce

Makes about 1 cup

¼ cup achiote (annatto) paste
Juice from 4 large oranges
8 cloves garlic, peeled
¼ teaspoon kosher salt, more to taste
¼ teaspoon fresh cracked black pepper, more to taste

Yucatecan-Style Redfish Wrapped in Banana Leaves

4 boneless red snapper fillets or other redfish
6 banana leaves (see page 12)

1 green bell pepper, seeded and sliced
1 red onion, peeled and thinly sliced
1 Roma or plum tomato, sliced
Warm corn tortillas, for serving
Cooked rice, for serving
Habanero or other smoky-spicy salsa, for serving

To make the Citrusy Achiote Sauce: Add the achiote, orange juice, and garlic cloves to a high-powered blender or food processor fitted with a blade attachment. Blend until smooth and then season with the salt and pepper. Taste for seasoning and adjust, as desired. Set the sauce aside at room temperature until ready to use.

Place the fish fillets in a shallow dish or bowl and cover with the Citrusy Achiote Sauce. Cover the bowl and allow to marinate in the refrigerator for 30 minutes.

Preheat the oven to 350°F.

To prep the fish, lay a banana leaf flat on a prep surface, then place a portion of the sliced vegetables and a fish fillet in the center. Fold the leaf into a package, tucking in the edges and sealing it well. Repeat with the remaining leaves and fillets.

Set the wrapped fillets on a lined baking sheet and place in the oven. Bake for 8 to 10 minutes, until the fish is cooked through. Remove from the oven.

To serve, place a wrapped fillet on each plate and allow guests to unwrap their own. Serve with warm corn tortillas, cooked rice, and habanero salsa alongside.

BEVERAGE SUGGESTION

Simply put, Tikin Xic pairs beautifully with a well-chilled Mexican white wine like a Valle de Guadalupe Sauvignon Blanc or Blanc du Bois. These wines offer bright acidity and tropical fruit notes that complement the citrusy achiote and fresh fish flavors. If you prefer a traditional Mexican beverage, try a fresh, lightly sweetened agua de jamaica (hibiscus tea) or tequila blanco cocktail with lime and a touch of salt. These will refresh the palate and highlight the dish's vibrant flavors.

Belgian-Style Beer Mussels

with Pommes Frites & Garlic Aioli

Our Belgian-style mussels have stood the test of time: they are a testament to simple ingredients coming together in perfect harmony and have been on our menu for over two decades. Steamed in a rich, aromatic Belgian beer broth, they soak up the deep, malty notes of the brew, enhanced by garlic, shallots, fresh herbs, and butter for a velvety finish. Each bite is briny, succulent, and irresistibly flavorful. They are paired with our crispy, golden pommes frites; these hand-cut fries are cooked to perfection—crispy on the outside, fluffy on the inside—offering the perfect crunch to balance the mussels' tender texture. To complete the experience, we serve them with our house-made aioli, a silky, garlicky dip that adds just the right amount of indulgence.

Serves 6

Garlic Aioli

Makes 1½ cups

8 cloves garlic, peeled
½ teaspoon kosher salt, more to taste
2 large egg yolks
1 teaspoon red wine vinegar
Juice of ½ lemon
1 cup extra-virgin olive oil

Pomme Frites

Makes about 6 cups

4 to 5 russet potatoes (about 1 pound)
8 to 10 cups neutral flavored vegetable or canola oil, for frying
½ teaspoon kosher salt, more to taste

Belgian-Style Beer Mussels

1 tablespoon extra-virgin oil
½ cup peeled and finely diced shallot
3 pounds fresh, cleaned mussels
1 cup unsalted butter
1 (12-ounce) bottle Belgian red beer or any dark beer
¼ teaspoon kosher salt, more to taste
¼ teaspoon fresh cracked black pepper, more to taste

To make the Garlic Aioli: Mash the garlic with the salt in a mixing bowl, making it into a fine paste. Add in the egg yolks, vinegar, and lemon juice, blending with a whisk to combine well. Gradually add oil, a drop at a time, whisking constantly. As the mixture begins to thicken and look like mayonnaise, add oil more generously until you have incorporated the entire cup. Note: Alternatively, you can also mix the aioli in a food processor fitted with a blade attachment, gradually adding the oil with the motor running. Taste for seasoning and add more salt, if desired. The aioli can be prepared up to 1 week in advance, stored in an airtight container in the refrigerator until ready to use.

To make the Pomme Frites: Wash and scrub the potatoes clean with a brush. Once the potatoes are dry, slice them into thin sticks—about ⅛-inch thick for classic frites. Place the cut potatoes in a bowl of cold water and soak for at least 30 minutes, or up to a few hours. Note: This helps remove excess starch and makes them crispier. Drain and pat the fries very dry using clean kitchen towels or paper towels. Pour the oil in a deep fryer or heavy pot so that the oil sits about 2 inches deep in the pan. Heat over medium-high heat until shimmering, about to 300°F on a thermometer. Fry the potatoes in batches until crispy and lightly browned, about 4 minutes. Remove and drain on paper towels. Season with salt and serve.

To make the mussels: Add the oil to a large sauté pan over medium heat. Once the oil is shimmering, add the shallots and sauté for 2 to 3 minutes, until tender and translucent. Add the mussels, butter, and beer, and bring to a low simmer. Cover and cook just until the mussel shells open, about 5 to 7 minutes. Remove from the heat.

To serve: Ladle a portion of the mussels on a plate and add a side helping of Pommes Frites. Drizzle with a few spoonfuls of the Garlic Aioli and serve immediately, with additional aioli offered on the side for dipping, as desired.

BEVERAGE SUGGESTION

These signature mussels with pommes frites and garlic aioli are simply amazing with a Belgian witbier (white beer) like Hoegaarden or Allagash White. The beer's light body, citrusy spice, and gentle carbonation complement the briny mussels, cut through the richness of the aioli, and refresh the palate between bites.

Crab-Filled Fried Green Tomatoes

with Roasted Red Pepper Remoulade

Few dishes capture the spirit of Southern cooking quite like fried green tomatoes—and this version takes it to the next level. Another favorite on our menu for almost 20 years, this recipe pairs crispy, golden-fried green tomatoes with a fresh, flavorful crab filling and a bright, zesty red pepper remoulade. The balance of richness and acidity makes every bite crave-worthy. Best of all, it's also surprisingly simple to prepare.

Serves 4 to 6

Roasted Red Pepper Remoulade

Makes 1½ cups

½ cup coarsely chopped roasted red peppers
1 cup prepared or homemade mayonnaise
2 tablespoons minced celery
2 tablespoons minced green onions
1 teaspoon peeled and minced shallots
1 teaspoon peeled and minced garlic
1 tablespoon Creole or other spicy brown mustard
⅛ teaspoon kosher salt
⅛ teaspoon fresh cracked black pepper

Crab-Filled Fried Green Tomatoes

¾ cup fresh jumbo lump crabmeat
½ cup diced red pepper
½ cup diced green onions
¼ cup peeled and diced red onion
3 tablespoons mayonnaise

½ teaspoon lemon juice, more to taste
⅛ teaspoon kosher salt, more to taste
⅛ teaspoon fresh cracked black pepper
3 large green tomatoes
1 cup all-purpose flour
2 large eggs
½ cup cultured buttermilk
1 cup cornmeal
Neutral flavored oil, such as canola or vegetable, for frying

To make the Roasted Red Pepper Remoulade: Add the chopped roasted red pepper, mayonnaise, celery, green onions, shallots, garlic, and mustard to a high-powered blender or food processor fitted with a blade attachment. Blend until smooth. Season with the salt and pepper, adding more to taste, as desired. The remoulade can be prepared 2 to 3 days in advance, stored in an airtight container in the refrigerator.

To make the Fried Green Tomatoes: Add the crab, peppers, green onion, red onion, and mayonnaise to a small mixing bowl. Stir well to combine. Season with the lemon juice, salt, and pepper, adding more as needed, to taste. The filling should be rich, yet bright with zesty citrus notes.

Slice the green tomatoes into ¼-inch thick slices. Place about 1 tablespoon of the crabmeat mixture on a tomato slice, then cover with another slice of tomato to create a "sandwich." Repeat with remaining tomatoes and filling.

Create your dredging stations: Place the flour in a shallow dish. Whisk the eggs and buttermilk together in a second shallow dish. Place the cornmeal in a third dish. Bread the tomatoes by first coating them in the flour, then the egg-buttermilk mixture, and finally in the cornmeal. Place breaded tomatoes on a plate.

Preheat the oven to 350°F and place a baking sheet on the center rack. Add enough oil to a large frying pan so that it is about 1½-inches deep in the pan. Heat the oil over medium heat, until shimmering, about 350°F on a thermometer. Once the oil is hot, carefully drop in the tomatoes in batches and fry for about 1 to 2 minutes each, browning on all sides. Remove the tomatoes with a slotted spoon and transfer to the oven to finish cooking, another 3 to 5 minutes. Remove from the oven and drain on a paper towel-lined plate.

To serve, arrange the tomatoes on a platter and drizzle the Roasted Red Pepper Remoulade over top. Serve immediately.

BEVERAGE SUGGESTION

Sticking with the Southern theme, this version of fried green tomatoes pairs beautifully with a classic New Orleans Ramos Gin Fizz. The frothy, citrusy cocktail with hints of orange blossom and creamy texture complements the crispy, savory crab and tangy remoulade while refreshing the palate with its bright, balanced flavors—perfectly capturing the spirit of New Orleans.

Sea Scallop & Shrimp Aguachile

with Jalapeño, Cucumber & Lime

Aguachile is a classic Mexican seafood dish that originated from the coastal regions of Sinaloa. It is like ceviche but typically features raw seafood—often shrimp, scallops, or fish—marinated in a vibrant, spicy, and tangy sauce made with lime juice, chiles, fresh herbs, and sometimes cucumber or other vegetables. Unlike ceviche, where the seafood is left to marinate for longer, aguachile is served almost immediately after mixing, preserving the fresh, delicate texture of the seafood.

Serves 4

½ pound cleaned, top-quality sea scallops
½ pound peeled, deveined high-quality shrimp
¾ cup fresh lime juice
1 jalapeño pepper
1 English cucumber
1 clove garlic, peeled and smashed
¼ cup lightly packed fresh cilantro leaves
¼ cup lightly packed fresh flat-leaf Italian parsley leaves
1 tablespoon fresh mint leaves
½ tablespoon canola oil
2 tablespoons water
¼ teaspoon kosher salt, more to taste
¾ cup thinly sliced red onion
Tostadas or tortilla chips, for serving
Korean chili threads, for garnish, optional

Slice scallops crosswise into ¼-inch-thick pieces. Thinly slice the shrimp. Add the scallops and shrimp with the lime juice to a glass mixing bowl. Cover and refrigerate

for about 45 minutes, stirring occasionally, until the seafood begins to turn opaque. This is the aguachile.

While the aguachile is chilling, stem the jalapeño and coarsely chop, removing about half of the seeds. Slice the English cucumber in half. Seed and coarsely chop one half, then thinly slice the other half. Reserve all three and set aside.

Add the chopped jalapeño with half of its seeds, plus the coarsely chopped cucumber, to a high-powered blender or a food processor fitted with a blade attachment. Add the garlic, cilantro, parsley, mint, oil, and water, and blend until smooth. Season the aguachile with the salt, adding more to taste, as desired.

Drain all but 2 tablespoons of the lime juice from the seafood. Add 3 to 4 tablespoons of the aguachile and mix well, reserving the rest for another use. Gently fold in the reserved thinly sliced cucumber and the red onion. Adjust seasoning with salt, as needed.

Garnish with Korean chili threads, if using, and serve immediately in chilled bowls or glasses, with tostadas or tortilla chips on the side.

BEVERAGE SUGGESTION

When making these succulent scallops and shrimp with jalapeño, cucumber, and lime, try it with a light, crisp Mexican lager like Modelo Especial or Pacifico. The beer's clean, refreshing carbonation and subtle malt sweetness balance the bright citrus and heat of the aguachile, cooling the palate and enhancing the fresh seafood flavors.

SUGAR & SWEETS

Sweet endings are my favorite kind of celebration, and this chapter is where I get to play with spice, texture, and a little bit of the unexpected. Many of these desserts—like our beloved apple-raspberry crisp and the soulful bourbon bread pudding—have become staples at Salum, thanks to diners who just can't get enough and want to bring that magic home. I love pushing boundaries here, too, especially with such desserts as the heritage-rich flavors of Mexican chocolate pecan pie and sweet chocolate-date tamales. This chapter is a journey through textures and tastes crafted to satisfy every sweet tooth—whether you're after familiar comfort or a daring new flavor adventure.

Apple-Raspberry Crisp

with Cinnamon-Sugar Crumble Topping & Crème Anglaise

Our apple and berry crisp has long been a beloved favorite here at the restaurant. Tart Granny Smith apples and juicy ripe raspberries mingle with butter and sugar, creating a warm, bubbling filling that sits beneath a golden crumble topping. Served with a scoop of ice cream or a decadent drizzle of creamy vanilla Crème Anglaise, and it delivers pure bliss—one heavenly spoonful at a time. If you are using frozen raspberries, do not thaw them first, but add them to the filling while still frozen. Because frozen berries often have a higher moisture content than fresh ones, it may take a minute or two longer to cook your crisp. Just ensure that the filling is bubbling at the edges of the dish before removing from the oven.

Serves 6

Crème Anglaise

Makes about 3 cups

½ cup sugar
6 large egg yolks
2 cups heavy cream
½ teaspoon pure vanilla extract
⅛ teaspoon kosher salt

Apple-Raspberry Crisp

FILLING

8 Granny Smith apples
1 cup fresh or frozen raspberries
½ cup sugar

TOPPING

1 cup cold unsalted butter
1¼ cups sugar
1¼ cups packed light brown sugar
1¾ cups all-purpose flour
1 teaspoon ground cinnamon
1 teaspoon kosher salt

To make the Crème Anglaise: Beat the sugar and egg yolks together in a medium-sized bowl, mixing until thick and ribbons form, about 3 minutes. Set aside. Add the heavy cream, vanilla, and salt to a saucepan and heat over medium-high until the mixture is just about to reach the boiling point. Note: Look for small, frothy bubbles to appear on the surface of the cream, usually along the sides of the pan. Turn the heat down to low. Remove ⅓ cup cream from the pan with a measuring scoop. Slowly drizzle the hot cream into the egg-sugar mixture to temper the eggs, adding in small amounts and whisking as you go. Then pour the egg mixture into the saucepan and cook, stirring constantly, until the mixture is slightly thickened and coats the back of the spoon, usually about 3 to 5 minutes. Remove from the heat and pass the Crème Anglaise through a fine mesh sieve layered over a medium-sized bowl, pushing it gently through with a spoon. Cover the bowl with plastic wrap, pressing down on the surface to prevent a skin from forming, and chill in the refrigerator until ready to serve. Leftovers can be stored in the refrigerator for 3 to 5 days.

Preheat the oven to 350°F. Peel, core, and finely dice the apples on a cutting board. Place the diced apples, raspberries, and sugar in a medium-sized bowl, and mix until the fruit is fully coated in the sugar. Place the filling mixture in a 9-by-12-inch ungreased baking dish. Set aside.

To prepare the topping, cut the cold butter into tablespoon-sized slices. Add the butter, sugar, brown sugar, flour, cinnamon, and salt to a large bowl. Mix until fully incorporated. Note: Don't over mix; the topping should stick together when pinched between your fingers and be dotted with small, pebble-sized dabs of butter.

Pour the topping over the fruit in the dish and spread it out in an even layer. Bake the crisp in the oven for 20 minutes, until the top is golden brown and the filling is bubbling around the edges. Chef's tip: You should be able to easily insert a knife into the filling once the crisp is done. If the apples inside are still firm, continue to bake longer, checking the crisp every 2 to 3 minutes, until the filling is tender. Remove from the oven and allow to cool for 10 minutes. Serve warm with a healthy drizzle of Crème Anglaise spooned over the top of each serving.

BEVERAGE SUGGESTION

I like offering the apple-raspberry crisp with a sweet, lightly effervescent Moscato d'Asti or late-harvest Riesling. I find these wines offer bright acidity and luscious stone fruit and citrus notes that complement the tart berries and warm spices while balancing the creamy richness of the anglaise.

Crème Anglaise

Tips for Getting It Just Right

This classic custard sauce is all about control—low heat, constant stirring, and a little patience go a long way. Whether you're drizzling it over fruit, cake, or my Apple-Raspberry Crisp, this classic French sauce is all about finesse. Here's how to keep it silky, not scrambled:

- **Go Low & Slow:** Always cook over low heat and never let it boil—high temps will curdle the eggs.
- **Temper the Eggs:** Slowly whisk hot cream into the yolks to gently raise their temperature before combining.
- **Stir Constantly:** Keep the mixture moving to prevent sticking or overheating.
- **Know When It's Done:** It's ready when it coats the back of a spoon—run your finger through it; the line should hold.
- **Strain It:** For ultimate smoothness, pour the finished sauce through a fine-mesh sieve.
- **Cool Fast:** Set the bowl in an ice bath or in the refrigerator to stop the cooking and preserve texture.

Bourbon Bread Pudding

with Vanilla Bean Crème Anglaise

Bourbon bread pudding is a staple at Salum—a true indulgence that never fails to satisfy. The thick, hearty bread spends a few very important hours soaking up the rich heavy cream, sugar, and bourbon, before being baked to perfection. The result? A golden, crispy exterior that gives way to a soft, custard-like center bursting with deep, caramelized flavors. It's boozy, buttery, and downright irresistible.

Serves 4

Vanilla Bean Crème Anglaise

Makes 2 cups

2 large egg yolks

⅓ cup sugar

½ vanilla bean

1 cup half-and-half

Bourbon Bread Pudding

1 (10-ounce) loaf of ciabatta bread

2 cups heavy cream

⅓ cup packed light brown sugar

⅓ cup sugar

1 whole vanilla bean, scraped

¼ teaspoon kosher salt

1 large egg

1 large egg yolk

¼ cup Jack Daniels bourbon whiskey

To make the Vanilla Bean Crème Anglaise: Beat the sugar and egg yolks together in a medium-sized bowl, mixing until thick and ribbons form, about 3 minutes. Set aside. Split the vanilla bean lengthwise, scraping out the seeds and reserving both the bean and seeds. Add the vanilla bean and seeds, as well as the half-and-half to a saucepan and heat over medium until the mixture is just about to reach boiling point. Note: Look for small, frothy bubbles to appear on the surface of the cream, usually along the sides of the pan. Turn the heat down to low and remove the vanilla bean. Remove about ⅓ cup cream from the pan with a measuring scoop. Slowly drizzle the hot cream into the egg-sugar mixture to temper the eggs, adding in small amounts and whisking as you go. Then pour the egg mixture into the saucepan and cook, stirring constantly, until the mixture is slightly thickened and coats the back of a spoon, usually about 3 to 5 minutes. Remove from the heat and pass the Crème Anglaise through a fine mesh sieve layered over a medium-sized bowl, pushing it gently through with a spoon. Cover the bowl with plastic wrap, pressing down on the surface to prevent a skin from forming, and chill in the refrigerator until ready to serve.

Preheat the oven to 350°F.

Slice the ciabatta bread into ¼-inch thick slices, then arrange on a baking sheet. Bake in the preheated oven until lightly toasted on both sides, about 5 to 6 minutes. Remove and set aside to cool.

Add the cream, sugars, vanilla bean and salt to a medium-size pot and heat over medium-low heat, stirring until the sugars are dissolved, about 3 minutes. Remove from the heat and place in a large mixing bowl. Allow to cool for 5 minutes. Add the egg, egg yolk, and bourbon to the bowl, and whip with a whisk to combine. Place the bread slices in the bowl, turn to coat, and allow the bread to soak in the bourbon mixture in the refrigerator for a minimum of 3 hours, best if overnight.

Preheat the oven again to 350°F. Grease a large baking dish with butter. Remove the bread mixture from the refrigerator and put on a pair of plastic gloves to keep the mixture from sticking to your hands. Using your hands, tear the bread into approximately

1-inch-size pieces, layering the bread in the dish as you go. Note: If there is additional bourbon mixture at the bottom of the bowl once you've finished, pour it over the pudding in the baking dish. Bake for 30 to 35 minutes, until the top is golden brown and caramelized and the pudding is set.

Serve hot with a drizzle of Vanilla Bean Crème Anglaise.

BEVERAGE SUGGESTION

I'll admit, bourbon bread pudding with vanilla bean crème anglaise and a Carajillo—a classic Spanish coffee cocktail made with espresso and a shot of Licor 43 or good-quality brandy or rum—is a game changer. The warm, sweet, and spiced notes of the Carajillo beautifully echo the bourbon's richness and vanilla cream, while the coffee adds a bold, slightly bitter contrast that balances the dessert's sweetness.

Extreme Chocolate Cake

with Classic Chocolate Icing

Why do I call this an "extreme" chocolate cake? Because it delivers an intense chocolate experience—without a single ounce of actual chocolate. Instead, this luscious cake is powered by a generous amount of extra dark cocoa powder, which helps create a deep, rich, and perfectly sweet flavor. Every bite tastes like pure chocolate heaven.

Makes one 9-inch cake

Classic Chocolate Icing

Makes 6 cups

¾ cup room temperature unsalted butter
1½ cups unsweetened cocoa powder
3 cups confectioners' sugar
1 cup whole milk
1 teaspoon pure vanilla extract

BEVERAGE SUGGESTION

This extreme chocolate cake with classic chocolate icing is the perfect match with a full-bodied red wine like a California Zinfandel or a Banyuls from France. Zinfandel's ripe dark fruit and spicy notes complement the intense chocolate flavors while Banyuls—a fortified dessert wine with rich, nutty, and cocoa nuances—mirrors the cake's decadence and adds a luscious, velvety finish.

Extreme Chocolate Cake

2 cups sugar
1¾ cups all-purpose flour
½ cup unsweetened cocoa powder
1½ teaspoons baking soda
1½ teaspoons baking powder
1 teaspoon kosher salt
2 large eggs
1 cup whole milk
½ cup vegetable oil
2 teaspoons vanilla extract
1 cup boiling water

To make the Classic Chocolate Icing: Add the butter to the bowl of an electric mixer fitted with a paddle attachment and beat on medium speed until light and fluffy, about 2 to 3 minutes. Stir in the cocoa powder and confectioners' sugar. Then, with the mixer still running on medium, gradually pour in the milk and then the vanilla extract, beating until smooth, about 2 to 3 minutes. Reserve in an airtight container in the refrigerator until ready to use. Leftovers can be stored in the refrigerator for 1 week.

To make the Extreme Chocolate Cake: Preheat the oven to 350°F. Grease and flour two 9-inch cake pans.

Add the sugar, flour, cocoa powder, baking soda, baking powder and salt to the bowl of an electric mixer fitted with a paddle attachment. Stir together on medium speed to incorporate, about 1 minute. Add the eggs, milk, oil, and vanilla and mix again on medium for another 3 minutes, until the mixture is smooth and well incorporated. Stir in the boiling water with a spoon, mixing well. Pour the batter evenly into the two prepared pans.

Bake for 30 to 35 minutes in the preheated oven until a toothpick inserted comes out clean. Cool for 10 minutes before removing from pans. Then, cool the cakes completely on a wire rack, for at least 30 minutes and up to a couple of hours.

Remove the reserved Classic Chocolate Icing from the refrigerator and allow it to sit out to soften for about 10 minutes. Using a knife, cut the cooled cakes in half horizontally, creating 4 even layers of cake. To assemble the cake, spread about ¼ cup of the frosting out on a large cake plate or serving tray, then place a cake layer on the plate. Spread about 1 cup frosting on top in an even layer using a flat angled spatula. Repeat with the 2 other layers of cake, layering frosting in between each. Place the last cake on top and fully cover the top and sides with the remaining frosting.

Serve immediately or lightly cover in plastic wrap and reserve the cake in the refrigerator until ready to serve. The cake can be made up to 1 day in advance; allow to come to room temperature before slicing and serving.

Mexican Chocolate Pecan Pie

with Piloncillo Syrup

This Mexican chocolate pecan pie is made with piloncillo, this time in a creamy, dreamy syrup that boasts rich, caramelized notes. It also features Abuelita Chocolate, a beloved Mexican staple typically used for hot chocolate, which lends a deep, rich chocolate flavor with warm hints of cinnamon. The pecans add a delightful crunch, creating a perfect balance of texture and taste.

Serves 8

Piloncillo Syrup

Makes ½ cup

1 (6-ounce) cone piloncillo

½ cup water

Mexican Chocolate Pecan Pie

1 (9-inch) storebought prebaked pie shell

2 cups halved pecans, divided

3 large eggs

3 tablespoons melted unsalted butter ½ cup sugar

2 tablespoons good quality Tequila

1 cup chopped Abuelita Chocolate

Micro arugula blossoms, for garnish, optional

To make the Piloncillo Syrup: Add the piloncillo cone to a small saucepan along with the water. Heat over medium-low for about 3 to 5 minutes, until the piloncillo melts and creates a thick syrup. Reserve at room temperature until ready to use. Leftovers can be stored in an airtight container in the refrigerator for up to 2 weeks.

Preheat the oven to 375°F. Cover the bottom of the pie crust with 1 cup of the halved pecans, arranging them in a neat, even layer.

Add the eggs to a medium bowl and beat well. Add in the melted butter and whisk until the mixture is bright yellow in color and well incorporated. Add the Piloncillo Syrup, sugar, Tequila and chopped chocolate. Stir until all ingredients are combined. Pour the mixture into the pie shell. Neatly cover the surface of the pie with the other cup of pecans.

Place the pie on a heavy-duty cookie sheet. Bake for 10 minutes in the preheated oven. Lower the oven temperature to 350°F and continue to bake for an additional 25 minutes or until the pie is set. Remove from the oven and cool on a wire rack. Garnish with micro arugula blossoms, if using, and serve warm or at room temperature.

BEVERAGE SUGGESTION

I like to pair this Mexican chocolate pecan pie with Rompope, Mexico's spiced eggnog-like liqueur. Its creamy texture, warm cinnamon and vanilla notes, and gentle sweetness complement the rich chocolate, toasted pecans, and deep molasses flavor of the piloncillo syrup—creating an indulgent, festive pairing full of nostalgic warmth.

Sweet Chocolate-Date Tamales

with Cinnamon

We've all heard how labor intensive making tamales can be, but this recipe is more than worth the effort—set aside an afternoon to make these decadent, slightly sweet treats and you'll receive rave reviews from your guests all evening long. Beautifully balanced by warm, creamy masa, the tamales are rich with deep cocoa flavor, plus touches of sweet dates and fragrant cinnamon. Serve them piping hot with a scoop of vanilla ice cream.

Makes 24 tamales

14 large dry corn husks
2 cups Nestle Media Crema, divided
¼ cup sweetened condensed milk
¼ teaspoon ground cinnamon
1 (12-ounce) package of semi-sweet chocolate chips
1¾ cups masa harina flour
2 teaspoons baking powder
½ teaspoon kosher salt
½ cup room temperature unsalted butter
1¼ cups whole milk, plus more if necessary
1 cup chopped dates

Soak the husks in warm water for at least 1 hour or until they are softened and easy to fold. Drain and set aside.

Prep the tamale components: First, add 1 cup of the media crema, plus the sweetened condensed milk and cinnamon to a small bowl. Set aside.

Then, place the chocolate chips and the remaining cup of media crema in a medium saucepan. Heat over medium heat, stirring frequently, for 5 minutes or until the chocolate is completely melted and smooth. Remove from the heat and set aside.

Add the flour, baking powder, and salt to a separate bowl. Set aside. Note: You should now have three prep bowls set aside and ready to go.

Beat the butter in the bowl of an electric mixer fitted with a paddle attachment until creamy.

Then, with the mixer on medium-low speed, alternately add about a quarter of the cinnamon-milk mixture, a quarter of the chocolate mixture, and a quarter of the flour mixture into the bowl with the butter, repeating in a rotation until all have been incorporated, mixing well after each addition. The masa consistency should be a thick cake batter. Stir in the dates.

Using the back of a spoon, spread about a 1/4 cup of the masa mixture in the center of the lower wider portion of one husk, forming it into a rough square. Fold the right edge, then the left edge, of the husk over the masa. Fold up the bottom edge and fold over to make a packet. Repeat with the remaining masa mixture and husks.

Place tamales in a steamer pot fitted with a lid, arranging the tamales upright in the steamer rack and adding water to just below the steamer rack. Cover tamales with a damp towel and place the lid on the pot. Set the heat to medium-high and bring water to a boil. Once boiling, reduce the heat to low. Steam, adding water as needed, for about 1 hour or until the masa pulls away from the husks. Remove from the heat and allow to cool for 5 minutes before handling. Serve warm with vanilla ice cream.

BEVERAGE SUGGESTION

These sweet chocolate-date tamales make an excellent pairing with a classic atole, especially a cinnamon or vanilla-flavored atole. The warm, thick corn-based drink complements the tamales' rich sweetness and spice, creating a comforting, traditional Mexican marriage that's cozy and deeply satisfying.

Tamales Dulces

A Sweet Spin on Tradition

When most people think of tamales, they picture savory bundles filled with pork, chicken, or cheese—but in many parts of Mexico and Central America, sweet tamales (tamales dulces) are just as beloved. Traditionally made during holidays or celebrations, these dessert versions showcase the versatility of masa and the magic that happens when it's combined with ingredients like cinnamon, dried fruit, chocolate, or even fresh berries. Unlike their savory cousins, sweet tamales often feature a fluffier, cake-like masa, sweetened with ingredients like piloncillo, condensed milk, or vanilla. They can be tinted with natural colors (like pink or yellow) and folded just the same—into corn husks and steamed until tender. This recipe takes the tradition in a rich, chocolatey direction with the warmth of cinnamon and the natural caramel sweetness of dates. It's comfort food meets indulgent dessert—and while it takes a little time, the result is a tamale that's creamy, soft, and perfect served warm with ice cream.

Tres Leches Cake

with Creamy Caramel

Tres leches is the quintessential Mexican cake, a vanilla sponge soaked in a mixture of three milks: condensed milk, evaporated milk, and regular cow's milk. This results in a rich, moist texture that melts in your mouth. To elevate its flavor, at the restaurant we top it with cajeta, a goat's milk caramel that adds a deep, caramelized sweetness to perfectly complement the delicate cake. A true celebration of Mexican flavors, this dessert is beloved for its luscious, indulgent quality.

Serves 8

6 large eggs
1 cup sugar
1 cup all-purpose flour
1 tablespoon baking powder
½ cup whole milk
2 tablespoons pure vanilla extract
1 cup heavy whipping cream
1 (14-ounce) can condensed milk
1 (12-ounce) can evaporated milk
½ cup storebought cajeta or other dulce de leche

Preheat the oven to 350°F.

Separate the egg yolks and egg whites, putting the egg whites into a medium-size bowl and reserving the yolks in a small bowl. Beat the egg whites until stiff. Gradually add the sugar to the whites in the bowl, stirring until completely incorporated. Add in the egg yolks one by one, whisking in between each addition. Add in the flour in small

increments, stirring as you go to incorporate. Stir in the baking powder, milk, and vanilla until the batter is nice and smooth.

Pour the cake batter into a 9-inch spring-form cake pan lined with parchment paper and bake for 25 minutes or until a toothpick comes out clean. Remove and let cool completely.

Add the whipping cream and milks to a bowl and whisk well, until the milk mixture is light and fluffy, yet still creamy, about 2 to 3 minutes. Pour the mixture over the cake, spreading evenly over the top. Cover the cake with plastic wrap and refrigerate for at least 2 hours, or preferably overnight, before serving, to ensure the cake fully absorbs the milk and becomes moist and tender. To serve, release the spring-form clasp and slice. Drizzle each slice with a few tablespoons of the cajeta or dulce de leche caramel.

BEVERAGE SUGGESTION

Tres leches cake and Licor 43, a smooth, sweet Spanish liqueur often enjoyed in Mexico, is a wonderful pairing. The liqueur's notes of vanilla, citrus, and warm spices echo the cake's milky richness and caramel sweetness, making it a luxurious and harmonious dessert pairing—especially served over ice or with a splash of cream.

ACKNOWLEDGMENTS

I've never been one to enjoy talking about myself, but one thing I know for certain is I wouldn't be who I am today without the people I'm about to thank:

Mom and Dad, you gave me life, love, and the gift of education. You gave me more than I ever dreamed possible. All I've ever wanted was to make you proud. Though you aren't here to see this book finished, please know every recipe and every photo in these pages is dedicated to you.

To Randy, my rock, my partner, my love for the past twenty-five years. Thank you from the bottom of my heart for your unwavering support, your patience, and for putting up with "Chef Salum" when he makes an appearance at home (our little inside joke—my alter ego isn't always the easiest to live with). I couldn't navigate this life without you.

To Alex and Leticia, my brother and sister, my partners in every twist and turn of life. Thank you for always standing by me, especially when things didn't go as planned. Your love and support mean the world. Thank you for giving me Gerardo, Celia, Fernando, Tanya, Sofia, and Santiago, the greatest gifts you could have ever given me. I love them all so deeply.

To my grandmothers, Lilia and Amira. Thank you for being such powerful forces in my life. You gave me the wings to cook freely, to trust my instincts, and to love the process. I adore you both endlessly.

To David Vazquez, my first love. You were the one who pushed me to follow my dreams, who stood by me through every wild adventure in our younger years. I credit so much of my courage to you.

And, of course, to my extraordinary cookbook team for making this dream a reality. To the maestro himself, James O. Fraioli at Culinary Book Creations, food photographer Alejandra Urquiza, editor Varsana Tikovsky, Alan Dino Hebel and Ian Koviak of The Book Designers, Jesse McHugh, and the wonderful team at Skyhorse Publishing, and Simon and Schuster. Thank you for your steadfast support throughout the process.

METRIC CONVERSIONS

If you're accustomed to using metric measurements, use these handy charts to convert the imperial measurements used in this book.

Weight (Dry Ingredients)

1 oz		30 g
4 oz	¼ lb	120 g
8 oz	½ lb	240 g
12 oz	¾ lb	360 g
16 oz	1 lb	480 g
32 oz	2 lb	960 g

Oven Temperatures

Fahrenheit	Celsius	Gas Mark
225°	110°	¼
250°	120°	½
275°	140°	1
300°	150°	2
325°	160°	3
350°	180°	4
375°	190°	5
400°	200°	6
425°	220°	7
450°	230°	8

Volume (Liquid Ingredients)

½ tsp.		2 ml
1 tsp.		5 ml
1 Tbsp.	½ fl oz	15 ml
2 Tbsp.	1 fl oz	30 ml
¼ cup	2 fl oz	60 ml
⅓ cup	3 fl oz	80 ml
½ cup	4 fl oz	120 ml
⅔ cup	5 fl oz	160 ml
¾ cup	6 fl oz	180 ml
1 cup	8 fl oz	240 ml
1 pt	16 fl oz	480 ml
1 qt	32 fl oz	960 ml

Length

¼ in	6 mm
½ in	13 mm
¾ in	19 mm
1 in	25 mm
6 in	15 cm
12 in	30 cm

INDEX

C

D

E

F

G

N

O

P